UNDERSTANDING PALMISTRY

Also in this series:

UNDERSTANDING PALMISTRY

How to read the map of life — in the palm of
your hand

by

Mary Anderson

Thorsons
An Imprint of HarperCollins*Publishers*

Thorsons
An Imprint of HarperCollins*Publishers*
77–85 Fulham Palace Road,
Hammersmith, London W6 8JB
1160 Battery Street
San Francisco, California 94111–1213

First published as *Palmistry:
Your Destiny in your Hands* 1973
This edition 1990
7   9   10   8   6

A catalogue record for this book
is available from the British Library

ISBN 1 85538 012 9

Printed in Great Britain by
HarperCollinsManufacturing Glasgow

CONTENTS

CHAPTER ONE

THE MAP YOU'LL NEVER LOSE

Palmistry has always had an unfailing amusement value. The hand reader is in demand at Christmas parties, to say nothing of the summer resort palmists, some of whom, within the limits of their own background, are surprisingly good. It is precisely this entertainment side of palmistry which tends to bring it into disrepute in scientific circles.

However, as with all the occult sciences, there has always been an esoteric or inner and an exoteric or outer body of knowledge; the latter fulfilling a definite human need to know the future and have answered such questions as: Will I get married? Be rich? Famous? Have children and be happy?

Rooted in Antiquity

But palmistry in terms of value goes deeper than this; its roots lie buried deep in antiquity. The ancient courts of kings had their wise men or soothsayers and they advised and warned from their knowledge of the stars and the signs and symbols which they read in the hands of men. In many countries, spiritual leaders were recognized by the signs on their hands.

According to the ancient teachings of occultism, man represents the microcosm — the small world — or the macrocosm — the universe. Everyone carries the map of their life in the palm of their hand — read aright it can unlock the mystery of destiny.

However, regarding the present position, Dr Charlotte Wolff, who has studied hands from the point of view of psychological diagnosis, answers most clearly the sceptic's query: Why should there be anything in it? She writes, 'The hand is a visible part of the brain.'

This then is the reply to those who are puzzled as to why the shape, crease-lines and markings of the hand should provide information as to the character, personality and abilities of a person.

So the real value of palmistry is to help us to know ourselves and in this way to develop our potentialities, recognize our limitations and so enable us to make the best use of what we have, directing our talents into ways of all-round fulfilment and happiness.

Control of Destiny

Palmistry can also help us in our human relations, to understand our relatives and friends. We gain insight through understanding and we may even be able to control our destiny by applying the knowledge gained with foresight to the understanding of all our human problems.

At the time of writing the medical world is taking an increasing interest in the study of hands and disease so that it is now possible to ascertain certain inherent weaknesses through the study of the hands of a new-born baby.

Dr C. G. Jung gave his approval to palmistry and wrote, '... the findings and knowledge are of essential importance for psychologists, doctors and educationists. It is a valuable contribution to a character research in its widest application.'

On a more everyday level this little book may help you to evaluate:

Your own individuality.

Your emotional nature — love, affection, sexual response, marriage.

Your success potential.

Your talents, creativity, imagination.

Your success in business and other enterprises.

Likelihood of fame, recognition.

Other indications to fulfilment, life experience, travel possibilities, spiritual development.

Destiny versus Free Will

In a book which deals with an assessment of personality through esoteric knowledge we always come up against the question of destiny versus free will.

It is the author's contention that certain factors are predestined; after all, so far as you know, you did not ask to be born. In palmistry, the left hand is always considered to be the hand of the inherited constitution and characteristics, and so the destiny we are born with; but the right hand shows the way in which our inheritance is used.

Those who are naturally left-handed must reverse this dictum.

So that while we live and have our being within the pattern of our destiny, our reactions to the blows or favours of fate are within our own control and it is to this extent that we control our destiny. It is only too true to say that our lives, and environment, material, physical and emotional, are but projections of our own natures.

Where we feel that we have been unfortunate we have to think about the necessity of change within ourselves, a willingness to change our attitudes, to be positive and courageous and experience life to the full. Only a change within ourselves will change what we are pleased to call 'our luck' for the better.

A fair understanding of palmistry can first of all give us insight into ourselves and others, secondly it can provide a great deal of interest and entertainment, thirdly, carefully studied over a period of years it can help in vocational guidance. It can be a guide to the choice of marriage partner, an aid in seeing how to handle and direct children, later can assist in planning their career and in medical circles can be used to indicate the early stages of certain illnesses.

In everyday life it can be helpful in understanding strangers, for as you study hands and gesture you will begin to get an insight into the person you are dealing with, whether this is an acquaintance, an employer or an employee.

Finally, it can become a lifetime study of great value and help you to develop not only insight, but also your ESP faculties and sensitivity.

CHAPTER TWO

FIRST STEPS

In order to be good at hand reading you have first of all to have a liking for people, then you must cultivate your powers of observation. You observe people, how they sit, how they stand and how they hold their hands.

Your first contact may be the handshake and this will tell you quite a lot about the person and the information you gain can be included in your reading.

The handshake can be firm, indicating a firm, positive, outgoing character; moist and clinging, showing an indeterminate, maybe weak type; a quick sharp squeeze, revealing someone who is often in a hurry and cannot bother to pay attention to the little things in life.

Watch and see how people hold their hands; note whether the hands give a relaxed easy impression when either placed on the chair arms or in the lap.

Do your subjects fidget with their fingers or with anything available? These are nervous, tensed up people.

Do they wave their hands about when they talk, illustrating everything with their hands? They are the

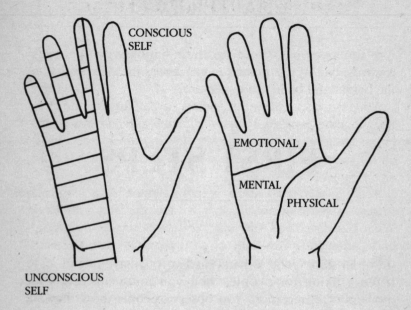

Fig 1 Areas of the Hand

voluble, talkative people who often 'tell all'.

Do they hide their hands or one hand in their pocket? These are people who are secretive or self-conscious.

While most people are only too anxious for you to read their hands, you will encounter the odd type who will firmly refuse and stuff their hands into their pockets, resisting the beguiling attempts of their friends to 'have a go'. These are the people who have deep-seated fears and one of these is that they might get to know themselves.

However, in general you will find that people thrust their hands at you palm up. It is wise, in order to avoid strain to the person, to find a table or something to rest the hands on while you examine them.

12

Routine for Reading Hands

Ask the person to hold up their hands with the back towards you. At this point you can assess the size relative to the height and build of the person.

You can also assess the spread of the fingers: are they held together, spread apart, or do they curl inwards to the palm? Is the index finger longer than the third finger? What about the thumb, is it long or broad? How is it held, close to the hand or wide apart?

Feel the hand for breadth, width, colour, shape, length of fingers. Are the fingers flexible or stiff? Are they knuckled? What basic shape is the hand and what are the finger tip and nail shapes? Are there any peculiarities as to the nails or the straightness or otherwise of the fingers?

Turn the hands over and examine the lines starting with the life line, the head line and the heart line, in that order.

Then examine the line of fate, the line of the Sun and the line of health.

Look at the mounts and their development and associate them with the relevant fingers.

Look at the mount of Venus, the girdle of Venus and the lines of affection to tell the tale of the affections, co-ordinating it with your assessment of the heart line and the general hand appearance.

Look for lucky signs on the hands, make your reading positive and encouraging. Look for the money signs, the 'lucky M' and the triangle and the angle of luck.

Finally, if you think that you see an adverse happening on the hand, never state baldly, 'It looks as if you'll have a serious accident at about 45', etc. The value of palmistry lies in warning and encouraging. More harm has been done by such Jonahs than can be truly assessed, and often the professional palmist sees the sad results years later.

Never Predict Death

If you see what you think is an adverse mark, whether it refers to accident or illness, put it tactfully and helpfully and *never* predict death. If you see what you think is an accident mark and the hand is generally of an impulsive type, you can warn by saying, 'I think you are inclined to take risks, you ought to be a little careful and watch this around the age of 25.' Adverse health indications can be handled by assuring the person of basic good health and vitality, but warning that at a certain age more care has to be taken than usual, and that a little more relaxation at that time would help.

Remember that it is the combined indications you see in the hand which will help you to arrive at the true picture. You are the artist who has to produce a portrait and you can only do this by combining the deductions you gain from the major signs and marks in the hand. Never go on one indication alone.

Always end on an encouraging note, for everyone has something to develop and some good fortune coming their way — stress this.

CHAPTER THREE

THE HAND

When we spoke about delineating the hand we advised you to look at the back of the raised hands. The shape of the hands is informative. Much can be gleaned as to temperament and characteristic behaviour.

There are five basic types:

The Square Hand

This really is more or less square and does describe its owner well, as in the modern parlance 'a square'. The palm is as wide as it is long, often the fingers are squarish, but they can be long or short and smooth or knotted. The owner of the square hand is a practical, down-to-earth individual, a realist.

He is a worker, essentially responsible and reliable, the 'salt of the earth'. His faults are that he is resistant to change, he can be a creature of habit, even dull, but on the whole his virtues of solid worth and achievement outweigh his failings. His are the hands of success and can belong to

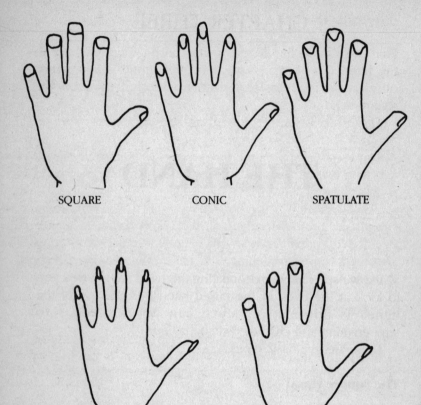

Fig 2 Hand Types

either sex, but are usually male. The businessman or woman or the good housekeeper both have square hands.

If there is a pronounced curve on the outer edge of the palm, these people are creative in a practical, constructive way. In general the square hand has few lines and these are straight.

They are people of integrity with no extremes.

The Conic Hand

The conic hand has round fingers and a rounded base to the hand. The fingers taper and the thumb often bends outwards. The lines show more variation than on the square hand.

These hands are often seen on the Latin races, also on the Irish.

The owner of the conic hand appreciates art and beauty and they make good hosts or hostesses, for the conic hand is basically female.

These people pick up knowledge quickly, but tend to be superficial, they are talkative, likeable and can influence others. With knotty fingers the conic hand owner may be of an original inventive mind, and have more staying power than the smooth-fingered folk.

The Pointed Hand

Often called the 'psychic'. This is a beautiful hand of delicacy and grace and it rightly describes its owners as such. The unfortunate part is that these people are relatively useless in the hard world of reality.

They are only partly of this world, the world never understands them nor they the world. They have an interest in the arts and often in psychic matters, but energy is lacking to produce anything creative. If the fingers are knotted, their lives are much luckier for they can become involved in the field of music, show business or anything to do with beauty culture.

The Spatulate Hand

This hand is narrower at the base than at the top of the palm. The fingers are broad (spade shaped) at the tips.

These are the hands of the individualist, the inventor and the mechanical genius. Science and engineering are their field and they love activity and travel. Their lives are subject to change and they do not in general make stable companions, but they are interesting company.

Women with this type of hand are firm believers in 'do it yourself'; they are always active and ingenious, versatile and capable.

The Mixed Hand

This is a definite type in itself and is often seen today, for it is the hand of versatility. The palm combines qualities of the foregoing types and the fingers are diversified. These hands combine creativity with practicality and are often found on the business side of the creative arts.

There are certain other factors to be assessed which may be mentioned briefly.

Hand Size

This must be judged in relation to body size, and assessment comes with experience. In general it can be said that the smaller the hand, the bigger the ideas and yet the less keen the person is on carrying out his ideas himself, especially if the hands are also smooth. The owner of the small hand thinks and acts quickly.

Large hands slow down a person's thought and action. A more analytical, thoughtful disposition is present, particularly if the finger joints are also knotted. These people like to carry out their own ideas.

The Handshake

This ideally should be firm and elastic, not *too* firm, for this shows that the person is trying to impress you. Nor should it be too soft and fleshy, for this shows a nature that likes luxury, can be sensual and indolent, and may want to lean on you.

A hard, dry hand shows overmuch emotional control; the person is probably self-centred, nervy and worrisome.

Hand Colour

The colour of the hands tell you about the vitality and activity of the person. Pale hands show lack of vitality — circulation is sluggish. Temperament is cool and there is lack of enterprise. The owner of the hand whose basic tinge is yellow often has a rather jaundiced outlook on life. Pessimism and caution colour the outlook.

The owner of the pink hand is in the happy position of being a normal, healthy, enterprising individual. With the owner of the red hand you have normal activity 'revved' up too much, there is too much push and go. The red hand shows an aggressive nature and overactivity.

Flexibility

The general rule is that the flexible, relaxed hand which bends backwards and forwards easily at the wrist and whose fingers are not stiff and unbendable belongs to the adaptable, easygoing, companionable, progressive person. The stiffer the hands and fingers the less easily accepting is the person. A stiff *hand* often shows a stiff *mind*.

Skin Texture

A fine skin shows a finer, more sensitive nature than is shown by a coarse skin texture.

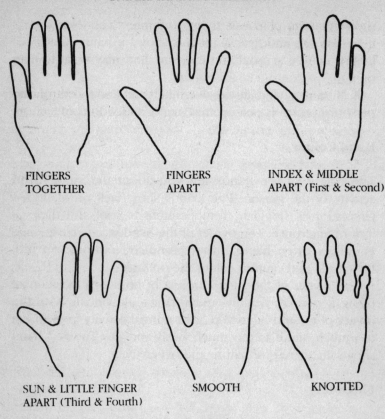

FINGERS
TOGETHER

FINGERS
APART

INDEX & MIDDLE
APART (First & Second)

SUN & LITTLE FINGER
APART (Third & Fourth)

SMOOTH

KNOTTED

Fig 3 The Hand Spread

Hand Spread

While you have the person's hands held up before you with
the backs towards you, you have the opportunity to glean
much from the way they hold the fingers.

1. If the fingers are held together, you have a person
who is very conventional and rather sensitive.

2. If the fingers are all apart then you can say here is an

unconventional person, who values freedom and is generous and rather bohemian.

3. If there is a space between the first and second finger then the person thinks for himself.

4. If there is a space between the third and fourth fingers then you have a person who values freedom of action, especially in his private life — too conventional a marriage just will not suit.

5. If all the fingers fall in towards the palm, you have someone who is very tenacious and wants to hold on to people and possessions. He is reserved and careful moneywise.

6. A wide gap between thumb and first finger shows a generous, independent, outgoing character.

7. Knuckled fingers, that is where you can see the joints pronounced, unless this is caused by rheumatism or some other disease of the joints, point to the person who thinks a great deal. These people reason and do not act on impulse or inspiration as do those whose fingers are smooth.

Finally remember that in right-handed people the left hand is the hand of their private, inner life, the hand of the unconscious, the right hand of the outward self, the person they show to the world. You will often find that these are markedly different, namely that their attitudes differ as to whether they are dealing with their families or their employer and the general public. Naturally the reverse will apply if the person is left-handed.

CHAPTER FOUR

ALL ABOUT THE FINGERS

Many points of value to be gathered from observation of the fingers are dealt with in the last chapter, for palmistry is above all good observation plus learning the meaning of what you observe about the way the person holds his hands, the shape of the hands, fingers and the markings on the palm.

Probably the thing that you notice first about the fingers is whether they are too long or short in relation to the palm.

This gives you an important piece of information about the person for it indicates broadly whether a person is an intellectual, emotional or material/physical thinker.

You can take it that the fingers are long in relation to the palm when the longest finger is as long as the palm itself. It is considered normal if the longest finger is about seven-eighths the length of the palm.

Short fingers are of course shorter than this in relation to the palm and with experience you will get to know whether they fall under the heading of emotional or material/physical thinking.

Long fingers point to a capacity for abstract thought, detail and exactitude.

Short-fingered people are quicker in thought, more impatient of detail, they see things as a whole.

With long, slim fingers the intellect is in control, with short, strong fingers the emotional/physical nature rules.

Smooth fingers are the fingers of intuition and inspiration, knotty fingers always imply analysis, criticism and a less companionable nature, however their owners gain in stability and a more serious outlook on life.

Thick fingers, like thick hands, show emotional force and energy, and fingers which are thick and fleshy as they emerge from the palm show that their owners like the delights of the table and are luxury lovers in general.

Finger length has also to be considered in the relation of one finger to others on the hand.

The Index Finger

This is also called the Jupiter finger. It is normal in length when it is equal in length to the third or Apollo finger, giving balance and confidence to the nature. If a little shorter it shows a person of some reserve, who is not inclined to boss others or too keen to take vast responsibility, but will work well in partnership and be quite happy sharing work and glory with others.

An index finger considerably longer than the third finger shows confidence and an outward-going personality. This person likes the limelight and has a tendency to dominate others.

A very short index finger shows a deep-seated inferiority

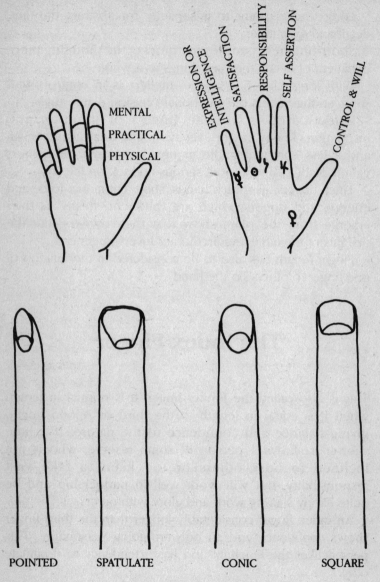

MENTAL

PRACTICAL

PHYSICAL

EXPRESSION OR INTELLIGENCE

SATISFACTION

RESPONSIBILITY

SELF ASSERTION

CONTROL & WILL

POINTED   SPATULATE   CONIC   SQUARE

Fig 4 Finger Types

complex, especially if it has also a long tie with the head and life line (of which more later in the chapter on lines), and a low set little finger.

In any case, a very short index finger always points to a cautious and retiring nature, while an index finger longer than the ring or Apollo finger gives extrovert and leadership qualities.

The index finger which curls in towards the middle finger shows a very retiring and self-effacing nature and even lack of pride and self-respect, for the index finger, being the finger of Jupiter, rules the good things of life and the ability to acquire them.

It is the finger of success, authority, happiness.

The Middle or Saturn Finger

This may be called the 'balance wheel' of the hand. It stands for responsibility in life and a person's attitude towards it. Over-long and heavy in relation to the other fingers, namely dominating the hand, it shows a serious outlook and foreshadows a life of many restrictions and responsibilities. These people do not attain success easily.

Straight and in proportion to the rest of the fingers, neither overlong nor overshort, it shows prudence and a reasonable attitude to life and its responsibilities.

The over-short Saturnian finger suggests a lack of inner strength and a certain irresponsibility. These people are often unconventional and some gravitate to the artistic or journalistic fields.

The Ring or Sun Finger

As mentioned earlier, when the Jupiter and Sun fingers are of the same length the character possesses balance and self-confidence. The Sun finger is the finger of creativity, art, success, fame and fulfilment.

A very long Sun finger, nearly equal to the Saturn finger points to the gambler with love, money, life. The person with a long Sun finger cannot live without excitement and stimulus.

A short Sun finger shows that the Jupiterian ambitions will dominate, the artistic and cultural side of life will be pushed to one side and the person will be always on the wheel of achievement.

A leaning of the Sun finger to the Saturn finger points to emotional immaturity, an unrealistic approach to love.

The Little or Mercury Finger

This the finger of self-expression, both mental and physical. It rules the intellect and professional and commercial activities.

The Mercury finger is normal in length when it reaches halfway up the nail phalange of the Sun finger. Self-expression is adequate, there is speed of thought and action.

If the finger is longer than this you find the person with a lively intelligence and a versatile, interesting manner of expression. If the nail phalange is the longest you have the writer and story-teller.

A short Mercury finger is a definite obstacle in life for we all need to be able to communicate adequately; it is specially difficult in marriage.

If you want to know whether a person is a good businessman or woman look and see whether the little finger curves slightly inward towards the Sun finger. This is the sign of a shrewd business brain.

In each finger the top section is taken as representing ideals and emotions, the middle section, mentality and powers of coordination, the lower section the material/practical and physical.

When doing a reading it is necessary to relate the affairs governed by the individual finger. If, for instance, you find that the third section of the middle finger is the longest then you know that the person is good at managing money, for the lower section of each finger deals with the practical and material spheres of life.

If the middle section of the Apollo finger is the longest, then in the sphere of art the business side of art and entertainment will attract.

Relate too the shape of the fingers to the meaning of each individual finger for you will sometimes find the mixed finger type, which is the versatile person, although normally the shape of the fingers should tally with the hand shape. That is to say that a square hand would ideally have square fingers, a pointed hand, pointed fingers, a conic hand, conic fingers, the spatulate hand, spade-shaped fingertips.

Square fingers show practicality and realism according to the affairs governed by that finger.

Conic fingers show impulse and imagination, again related to that particular finger.

Pointed fingers show artistic inclinations, intuition and often impracticality. These people are restless and changeable.

Spatulate fingers show energy, enterprise and originality.

A person with square tips on a square hand would be a very 'square' person indeed, a complete realist. A square hand would be improved by conic fingertips, giving a more imaginative and beauty-loving nature.

There is a saying in palmistry circles that 'fingers are best worn straight' and this is very true. Straight fingers show the person to be straightforward, honest and principled. If the fingers are spread wide the person is too outspoken, perhaps.

Crooked, the finger shows some deviousness — naturally unless this is due to accident and injury — in the affairs related to that finger.

When you have sized up the fingers for shape, size and section length, relate all these findings to the matters ruled by each finger.

Then look to see whether the fingers are spread wide or held close together when the hand is raised.

If spread wide, the person is more open; confident and freedom-loving.

If close together, the opposite holds — the person is reserved, close with money, lacking in confidence, secretive and rather conventional.

If the index and middle fingers cling, the person will achieve success through his work.

If the third and middle fingers cling, the person is insecure emotionally, rather immature and needs a prop. These people like to work in large organizations, for instance in either civic, governmental, the armed or nursing services. This gives them a feeling of belonging.

If the little finger stands apart from the hand the person needs independence workwise, and even within a close relationship.

The nails can give you some valuable information about the owner of the hand.

The square finger has a broad square nail, the conic finger has an oval nail, the pointed finger an almond-shaped nail, the spatulate finger has a nail with a narrow base which broadens towards the tip.

Short nails show the owner has energy, curiosity and intuition; broad nails show good judgement and clarity of thought. Long almond-shaped nails show less energy but the owners are more easy-going.

Pale nails show lack of vitality, coldness and possibly a selfish disposition. Pink nails show good vitality, warmth and a kindly disposition. Too red nails can indicate aggression.

The presence of moons on the nails is a good indication, showing a strong heart and good circulation.

Mr Johnson of Canada, an experienced palmist of many years standing, told me he had found something interesting relating particularly to the male which goes 'No moons, no stay' and can often be taken as an indication of the perpetual bachelor. With women it is said to indicate a dull marriage.

White spots on the nails indicate a tired and run-down constitution — there is need to let up and take a holiday.

Longitudinal ridges on the nails point to a tendency to contract rheumatism and an over-tense nervous system.

On the whole, sound nails of good colour indicate good health and temper.

CHAPTER FIVE

THE THUMB AND MOUNT OF VENUS

It is said that the Indian palmist can read the character and life story of his client in the thumb.

True or not, it is certain that the development of the human thumb has been closely linked with invention and technological development. Consider that anything which has to be grasped depends upon grip and the use of thumb power for conscious direction and it is the latter combined with will and reasoning power which the thumb stands for in the hand. For this reason it is the key to character and destiny.

Length: the thumb should be reasonably long. That is, it should reach well above the first joint of the index finger when laid close to this finger for measurement. Another guide is that the nail section should be the longest section in the hand, namely, longer than any of the finger sections, for this will give the person power of direction over his life.

The thumb should be firm, well-proportioned and moderately flexible.

The *angle* at which the thumb is normally held in relation to the hand is important. When the hand is spread out, the thumb should stand out from the palm at a reasonable distance, but not too far. A wide angle shows generosity, independence and love of liberty.

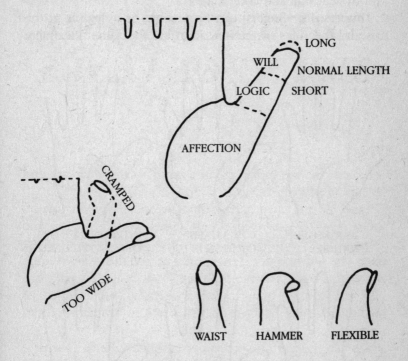

Fig 5 The Thumb

Too wide-angled a thumb shows a very asocial tendency, selfishness and a desire for complete freedom of action.

When the thumb is held close to the hand you have someone who is cold, selfish, close with money and also lacks independence.

The rule is, the larger the thumb the stronger the moral

force, self-control and intelligence. Small thumbs show a weak, impressionable nature.

The *set* of the thumb can tell you something important. The higher set the thumb, the less intelligent and the more selfish the person. A low-set thumb has a definite bearing on physical skill and coordination.

Thumbs, like fingers, can be flexible or inflexible at the tips and the rules of interpretation are the same. Flexibility

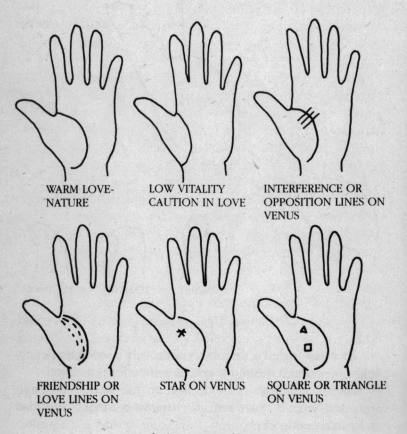

WARM LOVE-
NATURE

LOW VITALITY
CAUTION IN LOVE

INTERFERENCE OR
OPPOSITION LINES ON
VENUS

FRIENDSHIP OR
LOVE LINES ON
VENUS

STAR ON VENUS

SQUARE OR TRIANGLE
ON VENUS

Fig 6 The Mount of Venus

shows a sociable, lively, adaptable, easy-going nature. Stiff thumbs, like stiff fingers, show rigidity of mind, caution and reliability. The owners of flexible thumbs and fingers are observant and do well in jobs requiring observation and adaptability, like journalism.

Too supple a thumb shows the person to be too easily influenced by others.

The thumb is traditionally divided into three sections: the top, nail section representing will power; the second section, representing reason; the bottom section, which is called the mount of Venus, representing the love nature and the person's natural vitality.

When judging the thumb, the ideal is that the first and second sections should be equal, for a long first section and a short second section makes for impulse, while with a short first section and a long second section too much thought can choke action and so produce inertia. Such people are cautious and make good advisers for others.

A strong, full top section shows wilfulness and a 'me first' attitude. A thick second section does not make for tact or diplomacy, as the thin-waisted second section does.

Some time you may encounter the 'hammer thumb', a very thick first section and one can only say 'beware' for such people *can* be violent and in any case are extremely stubborn. In a woman's hand this can be a hereditary factor without any adverse psychological trait attached.

The mount of Venus is the third section of the thumb, that fleshy ball at its base encircled by the life line. It represents our capacity for love, including sexual love, friendship and our appreciation of beauty and the good things of life.

Men and women with a high, firm, full mount of Venus are highly sexed. To them love, marriage, the home and children are important. How the desire nature is controlled will be told you by the strength of the thumb and the head line. Unless there are other negative indications in the hand this is the hand of fertility and vitality.

A high, soft mount shows an excitable, changeable nature.

A small flat mount of Venus shows self-containment and detachment. A low vital force evidently does not allow them to give out much to others. This is not a good augury for a large family.

The shape of the thumb, like the shape of the fingers, also affects the attitude to life. Smooth-jointed thumbs show less thought than knotty ones.

Square-tipped thumbs show a realistic nature; pointed thumbs, especially if smooth too, show impulse and impracticality.

Finally, a high mount of Venus will give a hollow palm which — according to some palmists — is lucky since it has a holding capacity. To others it indicates over-caution, fear of life and a desire for non-committal, which in operation can lead to no life at all to speak of. But the hollow hand of the traditional palmists is a thin hand and should not be confused with the hollow hand caused by high mounts.

CHAPTER SIX

THE MOUNTS AND THEIR MEANINGS

Underneath the fingers lie the mounts — fleshy elevations — and palmistry traditionally assigns to them, as

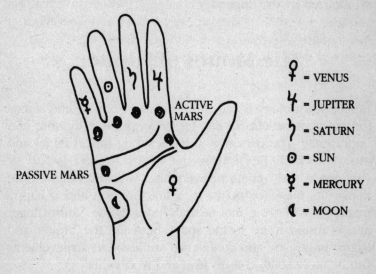

♀	= VENUS
♃	= JUPITER
♄	= SATURN
☉	= SUN
☿	= MERCURY
☽	= MOON

ACTIVE MARS

PASSIVE MARS

Fig 7 The Mounts

to the fingers, astrological names in keeping with the fingers whose base they form.

The mounts, by their development or the lack of it, by their firmness or flabbiness and by their placement under or to the side of the fingers, show developed or under-developed traits of character and lines of interest.

If developed, the special quality attached to that particular mount is strong in the nature. If the development is slight or non-existent, that particular trait or interest is latent.

Lines running to mounts tell you the special area of interest to which personal development and experience are directed. They are landmarks and save you from scratching your head too much as to the meaning of a particular line or marking on the mounts, that is, if you have firmly in your head the meaning of the particular mount, and it is as necessary to know the meaning of the mounts as it is to understand the area of character and experience symbolized by the fingers.

The Mount of Jupiter

Jupiter in astrology is called the 'Greater Fortune' and stands for the great benefits of life, for pride, position, honour and opportunity. The person who has a strong Jupiter finger and mount (which lies below the index finger) is full of confidence and optimism. Everything will turn out well, he thinks. Its presence points to a fine position and a happy marriage. When the mount drifts towards the Saturn finger and is found more in the space between the Jupiter and Saturn finger, joy and confidence are less, but achievements can be more solid, conservative and worthwhile.

One can have too much of a good thing though and this

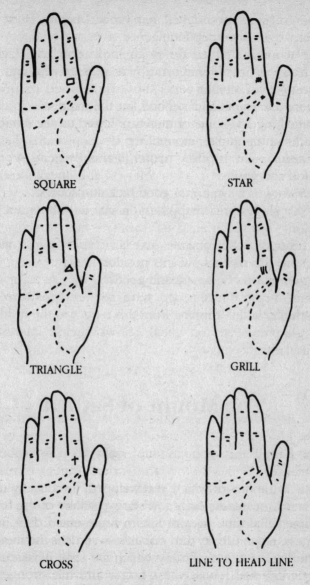

SQUARE

STAR

TRIANGLE

GRILL

CROSS

LINE TO HEAD LINE

Fig 8 The Mount of Jupiter

is shown by an over-developed Jupiter mount. High, soft and broad, it shows self-indulgence, a wastrel tendency.

A flat mount of Jupiter is an indication of a lack of generosity, of consideration, a lazy person who can lack self-respect or ambition.

There are marks and symbols on the hand which all tell us something and some of these are found on the mounts.

Marks on the Jupiter mount:

A *square* on Jupiter, protects the owner's worldly position and goods.

A *triangle* is a symbol of good luck and success.

A *star* shows great happiness in married life and a high position.

A *cross* shows a romantic love attachment which will in some way advance its owner's position in life.

A *grille* shows bossiness and egotism.

Since Jupiter has to do with money, position and opportunity, a line running from this mount to the head line (see Chapter Seven on lines), shows intense interests in financial advancement.

The Mount of Saturn

To be happy, this mount should really be conspicuous by its absence.

This is the mount which, if developed, lies directly under the Saturn or middle finger. When we spoke of the fingers we noted that the finger of Saturn represented duty, work, business, responsibility and stability — so does the mount.

The line of fate or destiny which we shall be discussing later is directed towards this finger and the stronger the line, mount, and finger of Saturn, the more restricted by

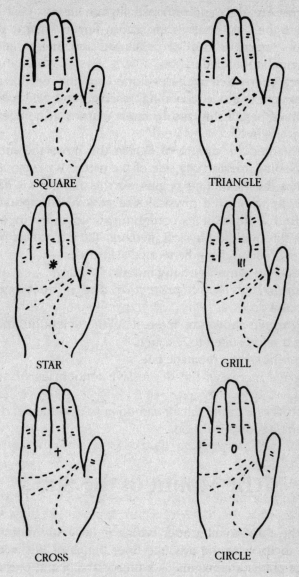

SQUARE

TRIANGLE

STAR

GRILL

CROSS

CIRCLE

Fig 9 The Mount of Saturn

temperament, duty and responsibility the life.

When the area beneath the Saturn finger is flat it shows that the Saturnian traits of pessimism and melancholy are not strong in the nature.

When there is a well-developed mount, we have the serious, introspective, brooding, reserved type. He has little warmth of personality and so rarely marries. If he does it is usually late in life.

The larger the mount of Saturn the more the morbid, introspective, melancholy side of the nature is developed.

When the heart line begins on this mount we have a person to whom the physical side of love is important as they find it difficult to communicate lovingly to others except through the physical medium. They are short on the niceties of life and can be termed selfish.

Marks and symbols on the mount of Saturn:

A *square* gives job protection and protects against financial worries.

A *triangle* shows an interest in the scientific and the occult, a mind suited to research.

A *star* hints at a dramatic fate.

A *grille* increases the depressive tendencies of a high mount.

A *cross* as a distinct mark can point to a sudden end.

A *circle* shows isolation.

The Mount of the Sun

Like the Sun finger under which it lies, this mount has much to do with the arts, the finer things of life, with the field of public entertainment, with sociability and prestige.

Well-developed, it indicates a pleasant, sunny disposition,

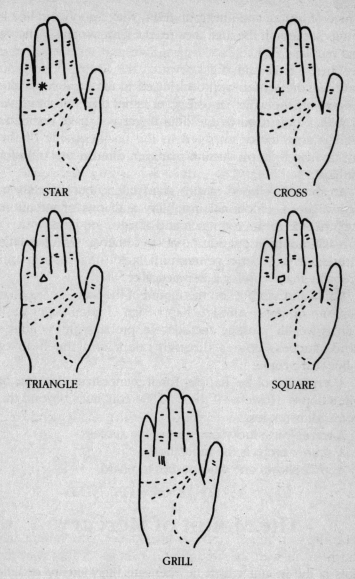

Fig 10 The Mount of the Sun

a love of beauty and artistic abilities. With a good Sun line it brings success in the arts: theatre, painting, writing, dancing and music.

When this mount drifts towards the Saturn finger you have a more serious approach allied to the creative faculty — possibly the writer or composer rather than the actor.

With a drift towards the little finger you have someone who is able for or engaged in the business side of the artistic field — a production manager, director or publisher perhaps.

An over-developed mount gives talent, but affectation, extravagance, emotional instability and love of attention. Such people dream too much and achieve too little.

A flat mount of the Sun points to someone who has little interest in aesthetic values and lacks imagination but probably makes up for it in practicality.

Marks and symbols on the mount of the Sun:

A *star* on the mount is a happy sign of good augur for it signals wealth, prestige and success, probably in the artistic field. Success comes through talent and the help of influential people.

A *cross* is not so happy, for it symbolizes dashing of one's hopes. However if the Sun line continues beyond this point, all is not lost.

A *triangle* is a lucky omen of stable success.

A *square* protects the reputation.

A *grille* shows one who pushes too hard.

The Mount of Mercury

This is the mount which lies beneath the Mercury or little finger.

Mercury in mythology was the messenger of the gods, so basically the Mercury finger and the Mercury mount inform us how a person will communicate. Although the Mercury finger is the smallest finger, both the mount and the finger symbolize many things largely to do with expression, such as writing, talking, selling, everyday practical and commercial affairs. They also symbolize science, business, health and the healing arts.

Since the Mercury finger lies in that part of the hand which is an expression of the instinctive self, the development of the Mercury mount and finger can also have a very large bearing on happiness in marriage and close relationships.

The well-developed, firm mount of Mercury shows a lively, practical, active person, someone who would do well in industry or business, especially anything to do with travel and communications.

With a good, but slightly curved inward Mercury finger we have the shrewd business brain, someone who makes money. To the strongly Mercurian type, variety is not only the spice of life, but a necessity.

Undeveloped, we have the impractical, muddled person, a person who is 'heavy on the hand'. Over-developed we have the 'con' man, who likes an easy life and easy money — this is sure to be true if the Mercury finger is also crooked.

When the mount drifts towards the Sun finger, we have someone who has a practical interest in the arts. A possible choice of career would be in the antique field.

When the head line points towards this mount we have the collector of things and knowledge.

There are various signs and symbols on the Mercury mount which are of importance in hand analysis. Here we find the lines of marriage and children, also the medical

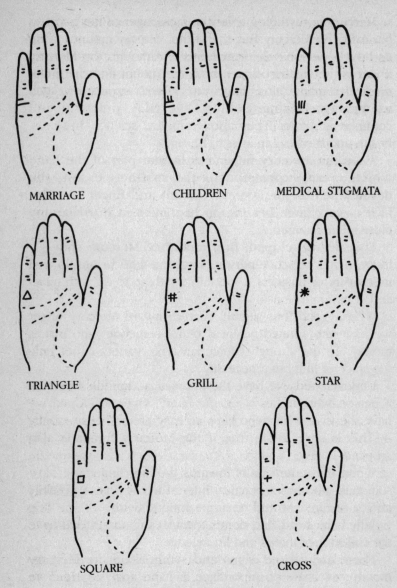

Fig 11 The Mount of Mercury

stigmata, consisting of a few straight, short lines. With a good Mercury finger and the rest of the fingers also good and thick, we have the indications of one who would make a doctor, nurse or social worker. The presence of the medical stigmata also shows one who is sympathetic and will help others in need.

Minor marks on the mount:

A *triangle* shows success in business.

A *grille* points to cunning or dishonesty.

A *star* points to success in examinations as a scientist or inventor.

A *cross* can mean double dealing and is a warning against this from others.

A *square* shows protection against mental strain.

From the Mercury mount starts the line of health and success in business.

The Mount of the Moon

The mount of the Moon lies on the far side of the hand and opposite the thumb.

You can see whether this mount is developed or not by the fact that the outer edge of the palm will curve if it is and this is always called the creative curve, for the mount of the Moon is the area of imagination and creativity.

A firm, developed mount of the Moon denotes sensitivity and a fertile, creative imagination. The line of the Sun usually begins in this area and shows imagination leading to success in the creative field.

Lines of travel and of restlessness are also marked on the mount of the Moon, when the person voyages in imagination or in fact to faraway places.

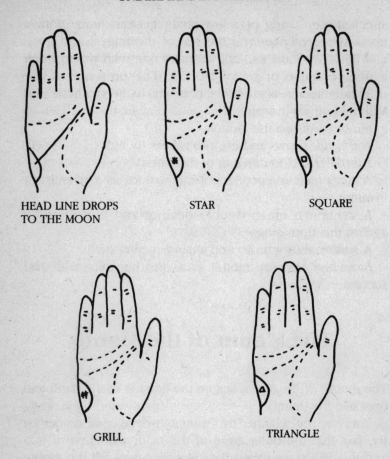

HEAD LINE DROPS
TO THE MOON

STAR

SQUARE

GRILL

TRIANGLE

Fig 12 The Mount of the Moon

Where you find a high, soft, over-developed mount of the Moon you will find the moody, touchy, changeable person who lives in his dreams and whose emotional relationships are always up and down due to his own inconstancy.

A flat mount (a hand where the edge is straight up and down) indicates that there is less imagination, sympathy and warmth. These people tend to get set in their ways mentally and physically early in life and stay so.

When the mount of Luna drops into the wrist the person has an awareness of rhythm in life and nature.

Sometimes the head line dips towards the mount of the Moon. Here we have creativity and imagination for use, as in the writer or artist.

The head line should not dip too far though or there will be too much dreaming and disconnection with reality, which can lead to mental instability.

Minor marks on the mount:

A *star* on the mount shows brilliant imagination.

A *square* gives protection in travel.

A *grille* shows worries and imaginary fears.

A *triangle* on the hands of a creative person shows success.

The Mounts of Mars

There are two Mars mounts and as Mars is the god of war, we have one which shows active courage and aggression, the will to fight, and the other which shows the more passive side of Mars, endurance.

The active, lower mount of Mars lies beneath the mount of Jupiter, above the thumb and below the life line.

With this mount strongly developed, we have the person with physical courage and plenty of fight; over-developed, it shows the quarrelsome bully. Flat, we have the coward.

The other mount lies above the mount of the Moon, on the outside of the palm, between the head and heart lines.

This mount developed shows self-control and over-developed shows bad temper and a sarcastic bent.

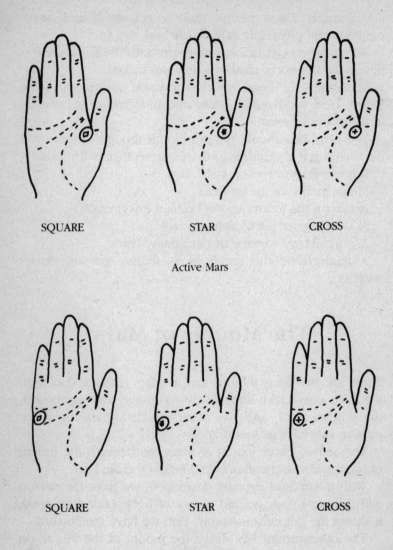

SQUARE   STAR   CROSS

Active Mars

SQUARE   STAR   CROSS

Passive Mars

Fig 13 The Mounts of Mars

An undeveloped upper mount again shows timidity.

The active or lower mount of Mars has a great deal to do with vitality, its moderate development adding to the vital force, therefore it is excellent for success in competitive sport.

A square on either mount shows protection from enemies, a star achievement from one's own strength of will. A cross shows secret or open enemies.

CHAPTER SEVEN

THE MAJOR LINES — YOUR PERSONAL MAP

The Life Line

The life line will be found on all hands. It begins at the edge of the palm between the thumb and index finger and encircles the Venus mount, the fleshy pad at the base of the thumb.

Its beginning, the length and depth of its marking, and whether it is broken, crossed or chained will tell you about the vitality and possibly longevity, although depth and strength of the line taken with other factors showing vitality in the hand, such as the Venus and Mars mounts, may often mean more than a very long line completely encircling the Venus mount.

Especially strengthening is a line which follows it closely, sometimes for quite a long way. This is known as a Mars line and gives additional strength and resistance.

Likewise if the life line forks at the base, again this is a sign of strong resistance to disease.

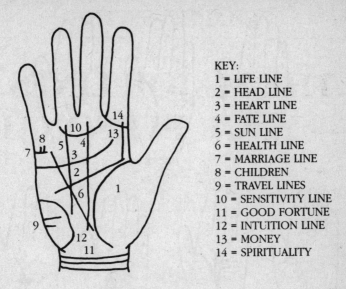

KEY:
1 = LIFE LINE
2 = HEAD LINE
3 = HEART LINE
4 = FATE LINE
5 = SUN LINE
6 = HEALTH LINE
7 = MARRIAGE LINE
8 = CHILDREN
9 = TRAVEL LINES
10 = SENSITIVITY LINE
11 = GOOD FORTUNE
12 = INTUITION LINE
13 = MONEY
14 = SPIRITUALITY

Fig 14 The Major Lines

However, you can take it that if you see a long, clear life line, free from chains, breaks and islands, then the owner has plenty of vitality and a strong constitution and is likely to make old bones.

The sweep of the life line is important, showing far more force and drive than when the life line comes down straight and so narrows the space of the Venus mount.

The beginning of the life line gives valuable information about character and life approach. The normal beginning to the life line is under the mount of Jupiter, but if it begins *on* that mount then the person is extremely ambitious and — unless the thumb and head line are weak — will reach his life goals.

Since markings on the life line show events and forces which affect the life for good or ill it is wise to know when to expect them, then it is possible to look forward to the

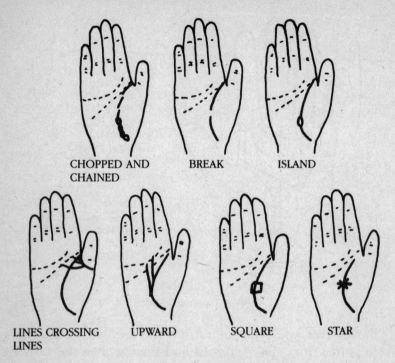

CHOPPED AND CHAINED   BREAK   ISLAND

LINES CROSSING LINES   UPWARD   SQUARE   STAR

Fig 15 Markings on the Life Line

good happenings and to ease the brunt of the more difficult.

The hand seems to go along with the biblical 'three score years and ten' and 70 years on the life line is about an inch above the thick base of the palm.

The easiest way to find time on the life line is to divide it up into 10-year sections, remembering that the line starts under the Jupiter mount so that your first three divisions will represent youth — up to 30 years of age — the next three divisions will carry you through the middle years and the last 10 years will represent age. If the line continues past your 70 mark then longevity is indicated.

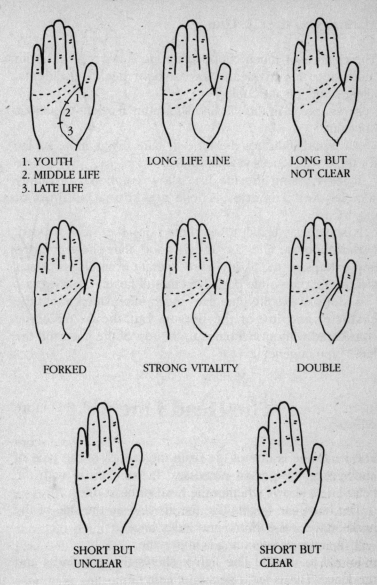

1. YOUTH
2. MIDDLE LIFE
3. LATE LIFE

LONG LIFE LINE

LONG BUT
NOT CLEAR

FORKED

STRONG VITALITY

DOUBLE

SHORT BUT
UNCLEAR

SHORT BUT
CLEAR

Fig 16 Type of Life Line

Markings on the Life Line

The chained or much chopped up life is not a good health indication. It can mean general poor health, accidents, allergies or spinal trouble.

A real break in the life line shows an accident or serious ill-health.

An island indicates the time to take things more easily, for there will be less vital force.

Lines crossing the life line show emotional or family worries and anxieties. These are known as lines of experience.

A square, as usual, gives protection when it is needed. Upward moving lines are always good, they show progress and enterprise, the ability to recuperate from illness. A star always indicates a life crisis, whether of health or progress.

A study of the life line gives much information about the character and life of the person, but should never be considered without reference to the rest of the lines and the hand type in general.

The Head Line

The head line is one of the main indications of the type of intelligence the person possesses. In comparison with the heart line it shows whether the head or heart rules.

The head line begins like the life line on the side of the hand between the thumb and index finger.

Its manner of beginning is important:

Joined to the life line lightly shows thoughtfulness and prudence. This is not a person of extremes.

Joined to the life line for about half-an-inch shows the

ultra-cautious, rather fearful person who follows the teachings of his elders and the majority way of thinking. He is usually slow to make changes and lacking in confidence.

Where you find the head line separated narrowly from the life line, you have a more enterprising, confident, original way of looking at life — these people can and do take risks; they are impulsive.

Where the life line and the head line are widely separated in both hands it suggests recklessness, extreme impulse and restlessness. These people find it hard to stick at anything for long.

Where the head line starts just inside the life line on the mount of Mars, you have a sensitive, excitable and touchy character.

You may find that a person has one indication on one hand and another on the other, in which case there will always be conflict, one side of the nature pulling against the other. The person will exhibit traits of independence at one time and extreme lack of confidence in other situations.

When assessing the head line, it is wise to remember that all straight lines show control so a short straight line will show a basically practical, shrewd mind. Many businessmen have these.

A long, straight head line will show preoccupation with detail and a capacity to organize and control the mind to given ends, in fact the ability to concentrate.

It is true to say that the average man has a curved heart line and a straight head line, while the reverse holds true for the average woman.

The curving down of the head line shows imagination and intuition and we all know about 'women's intuition', which also bears out the fact that in general women have sloping headlines.

On the square, practical hand you will usually find the

straight head line showing an excellent logical, realistic mind, and when you find a sloping one you can say that the person will use his or her intuitive, creative gifts in a practical and constructive manner.

The conic hand usually has a sloping head line so if you find that there is a straight head line, then the usual flair for self-expression, the creative and inventive turn of mind shown by the conic hand will be much muted and turned to more mundane, practical or technical matters.

Where you find a wide fork at the end of the sloping head line, you will find a person who is too versatile and who lacks concentration and single-mindedness.

The same applies if you have the end of the line split into several branches — the person tends to be muddled and confused.

Events can be timed on the head line as on the life line, but it is easiest in this case to divide the line up into three sections for youth, adulthood and later life beginning with the start of the line on the palm between the thumb and index finger.

Markings on the Head Line

A light and wavery line shows lack of direction, difficulty in concentrating.

A chained head line shows worry, anxiety and tension at the time shown by the chains or islands.

A break in the head line can show a breakdown, but if enclosed by a square or if the line overlaps, recovery. Little lines crossing show worries and maybe headaches. A line reaching up from the head line to the heart line shows the likelihood of an unhappy experience in love, hence from then on a much more hardheaded approach to life.

Many successful people have this line, which marked a

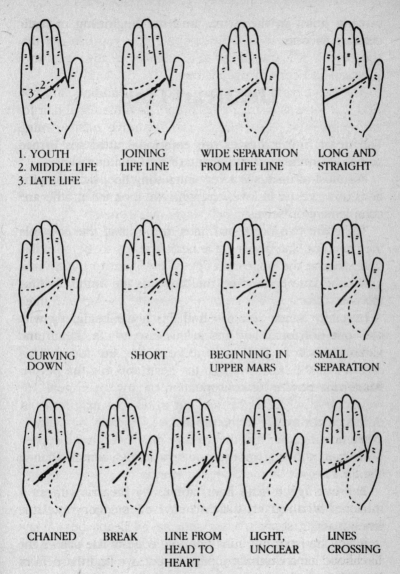

Fig 17 Types of Head Line

turning point in their lives and the beginning of their outward success.

The Heart Line

The heart line indicates the emotional attitudes in the person, warmhearted and giving or cold and introverted.

For most of us this is a very interesting line, showing as it does how we are in love, and what we look for in others to complement ourselves.

There are two horizontal lines in the hand, the lower is the head line, the upper is the heart line.

It starts at the opposite edge of the palm to the thumb, under the little finger, and runs towards the thumb side of the palm.

In a few hands you will find this line missing, there is only one horizontal line and in this case it is the head line, namely the head line and the heart line are fused. This shows that the head will rule the heart and that the person has terrific powers of concentration on any given goal. He will achieve whatever he sets out to do, but may lose out on his emotional life in the process.

We noted earlier that the average male hand has a curved heart line, showing more impulse and less control than a straight one.

The average female hand shows by its straightness a more controlled attitude to love, a slower reaction emotionally.

When the heart line runs from the edge of the palm right across the hand onto the Jupiter mount, we find the person who is possessive in love.

When the heart line curves upwards and finishes

THE MAJOR LINES — YOUR PERSONAL MAP

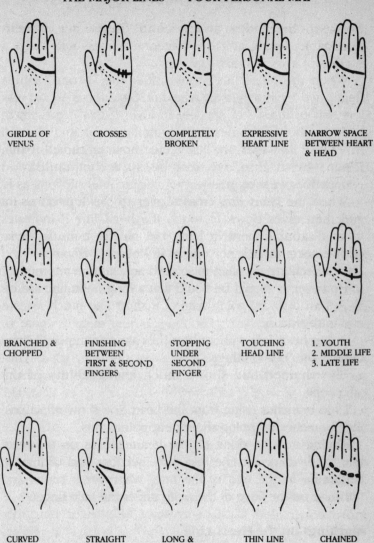

GIRDLE OF
VENUS

CROSSES

COMPLETELY
BROKEN

EXPRESSIVE
HEART LINE

NARROW SPACE
BETWEEN HEART
& HEAD

BRANCHED &
CHOPPED

FINISHING
BETWEEN
FIRST & SECOND
FINGERS

STOPPING
UNDER
SECOND
FINGER

TOUCHING
HEAD LINE

1. YOUTH
2. MIDDLE LIFE
3. LATE LIFE

CURVED
HEART
STRAIGHT
HEAD

STRAIGHT
HEART
& CURVED
HEAD

LONG &
STRAIGHT

THIN LINE

CHAINED

Fig 18 Types of Heart Line

between the index and second finger, we have a reasonable, loving attitude, someone who should make a success of love and marriage.

When the heart line stops under the second, Saturn finger, we have a person who finds it difficult to express any sort of finesse or subtlety in love. If this is present in both hands then the person is naturally selfish and physical in love. If however, the left hand shows a curved, much longer heart line, we can be sure that childhood experiences were repressive.

When the heart line crosses over to the Jupiter mount and then dives down to touch the head line it indicates great disappointment in love, but chiefly because these people seem to lack perception in knowing whom to love. Their affections are often misplaced and seldom returned.

However, it should be noted that a long heart line always shows an outward-going nature, a short line much reserve and introversion.

A thin heart line without branches shows the person who does not go out to others.

The chained line shows much changeability of the affections.

Little branches rising from the heart line show affections, little branches dropping show disappointments.

Timing may be done on the heart line as on the head line by dividing the line into three sections and taking the beginning as the end of the line, wherever it starts, and finishing on the edge of the palm under the little finger.

Markings on the Heart Line

Some hands have what is called a girdle of Venus, which is a semi-circular line, broken or unbroken, running above the heart line and below the fingers. This is an indication of great sensitivity and is really an addition to the heart line. This girdle is often present when there is only a single horizontal line in the hand and this shows a much warmer nature and the capacity to feel affection.

Crosses and breaks on the heart line show emotional sorrows, sometimes the loss of a lover or the end of an affair. A completely broken heart line shows a very demanding nature.

While the heart line shows your approach to other people and your way of expressing affection, it also shows something more, your appreciation of the arts and your creative capacity. An artist, for instance, may have quite a short head line, but an expressive, well-marked, branched heart line.

Do you relate everything in life to yourself? This is shown by the space between the two horizontal lines. Narrow space, self-centred and narrow in outlook, wide space, breadth of mind and vision.

These three lines, life, head and heart, are the major lines of the hand, but there are three other lines which are often found and can be easily located once you have found the three major ones.

The Fate Line

The fate line generally starts at the base of the hand, near the wrist and proceeds up the palm to the base of the second finger.

When the fate line exists at all it indicates that the person has a direction and purpose in life, is in control of his own destiny and is responsible.

The absence of this line tells of lack of direction or pur-

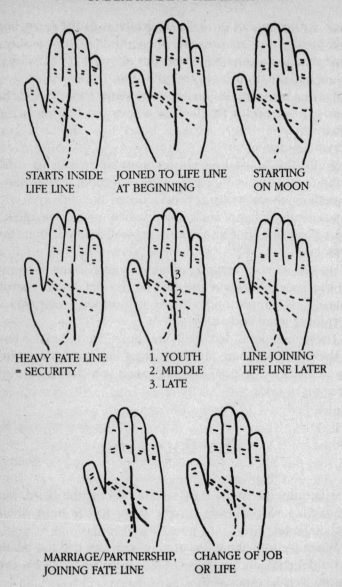

STARTS INSIDE
LIFE LINE

JOINED TO LIFE LINE
AT BEGINNING

STARTING
ON MOON

HEAVY FATE LINE
= SECURITY

1. YOUTH
2. MIDDLE
3. LATE

LINE JOINING
LIFE LINE LATER

MARRIAGE/PARTNERSHIP,
JOINING FATE LINE

CHANGE OF JOB
OR LIFE

Fig 19 Types of Fate Line

pose, an inability to fit in with the demands of society and therefore an irresponsible, changeable life; the person is like a twig blown about by every current. It is very important to help a young person who has no fate line to find a true interest and direction otherwise he will waste his time and talents in fruitless activities. He will be a real rolling stone.

The fate line does not always begin at the wrist; it can have other beginnings and can be long or short.

Beginning inside the life line it indicates help from parents to get ahead in life.

Joined to the life line at the beginning means great family attachment and maybe sacrifice for the parents.

Beginning on the mount of the Moon, opposite the base of the thumb, we have the person whose career is much subject to public approval, maybe the entertainer or the politician, someone who both gains and needs approval.

The person in whose hand the fate line runs up deep and heavy from wrist to the mount of Saturn is a very independent type. He makes his own decisions and they are always responsible ones. He does not like change, he is an exponent of all that is most responsible in human nature, he loves and craves security.

If this line cuts the hand in half, so heavy is it, then the person tends to get in a rut.

From the fate line you can read your life and by dividing the line into three you can time your changes.

Take from the base of the hand to the first horizontal line as marking 1 to 30, the youthful years, take from the lower horizontal line to the higher as marking the middle period up to about 45, take from the upper horizontal line to the base of the fingers as indicating the years from 45 onwards. Dividing these into sections of 10 again will help you time your changes of destiny pattern.

More About the Fate Line

The fate line running from the base of the wrist up to the mount of Saturn below the middle finger shows a person who will always opt for security. In a man this often shows a long career with the same firm. He will work hard, raise a family and retire to enjoy a well-merited pension.

Similar markings on a woman's hand may indicate the same, but are more likely to indicate a comfortable, secure marriage.

Where the fate line is joined to the life line at the start then there is a strong family attachment, or this can mean in these days an attachment to a community way of living. In any case the young person does not want to leave the group, he wants to belong. When the life line leaves the fate line, he finally gains independence.

The fate line which starts on the mount of the Moon opposite the base of the thumb will be found on the hands of those who depend for their livelihood on the impression they are able to make on the minds and emotions of the masses, that is they work in a personal way with the public.

When the line starts clear at the wrist, then joins the life line later on, it shows a sacrifice of personal wishes and career for parents or relatives. When the line clears from the life line the person is able to pursue his own life again.

Marriage or partnership is shown by a line which joins the line of destiny from the mount of the Moon side of the hand.

Changes in job or career can be seen by a break in the destiny line and if the lines overlap this will be a successful change.

A branch from the fate line running to the ring or Apollo finger shows success in the artistic field.

Markings on the Fate Line

Lines crossing the fate line show obstacles to be overcome.

Islands or breaks in the fate line show trouble and uncertainty.

Squares on the fate line, as elsewhere, show protection from the worst that fate can do for you.

If the fate line doubles, then you have a time of good fortune; this can mean marriage or money or both. In any case you will not be alone.

The Sun Line

The line of the Sun or Apollo is often called the line of success and the least that it can mean in a hand is optimism and satisfaction with one's lot in life.

Public renown can be seen by the line of the Sun which starts early in the base of the palm and runs up to the ring finger. This is the mark of the successful artist or entertainer. It refers to any accomplishment in the arts or in political life.

This line may be lacking in those who attain fame, but in some way their success will be bitter and they will lack what they feel they deserve.

There are many hands where the line does not start until above the heart line. This indicates that they find greater happiness and self-expression later in life.

Events can be timed on this line, as on the line of fate, by division into three sections as before.

Markings on the Sun Line

A long strong Sun line ending in a star or triangle destines

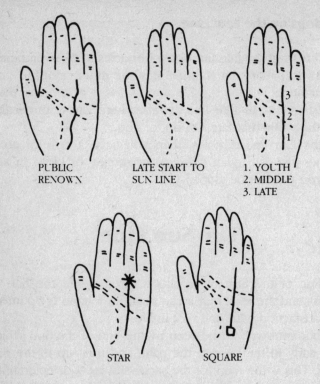

Fig 20 Types of Sun Line

its owner to fame and fortune. There will be tremendous public recognition of talent.

A square protects from any adversity or check to the public career.

The Health Line

Health is probably the most essential factor in the living of a successful and full life and this is borne out by the fact that in palmistry, as in astrology, the areas of health and work — hence material reward — are linked.

The line of health starts below the little finger and runs across the palm towards the base of the thumb.

Sometimes it joins the life line and if it is stronger than the life line at this point is will be a critical time for the person healthwise.

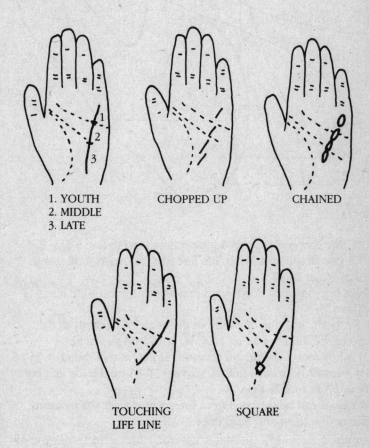

1. YOUTH   CHOPPED UP   CHAINED
2. MIDDLE
3. LATE

TOUCHING   SQUARE
LIFE LINE

Fig 21 Types of Health Line

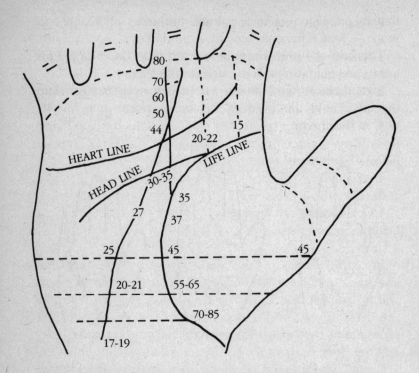

(i) A line dropped from mid-Jupiter finger to life line = age 15
(ii) A line dropped down to life line from between Jupiter and Saturn = age 20-22
(iii) A line dropped down from mid-Saturn finger to life line = approx 35-37
(iv) A horizontal line drawn from the angle of dexterity at the base of the thumb = 45 on life line, but 25 on the fate line
(v) A horizontal line drawn as above along base of thumb = 55-65
(vi) A lower horizontal line as above = 70-85 on the life line but about 17-19 on fate line
(vii) Lines can be dropped from fingers at intervals to measure time on the heart and head lines

Fig 22 Timing on the Hand

Points to note regarding the health line:

1. This is the line whose absence should bring us joy for it indicates that the person has sound health.
2. Unbroken and strong, it indicates good earning capacity, health and excellent business sense.
3. A chopped-up health line shows indifferent health and possibly — since it has been called the liver line — digestive problems.
4. Chained or islanded, there will be periods of ill-health at the time these occur on the line, maybe hospitalization.
5. A square shows protection either where business or health is concerned.

In timing events on the health line remember that the line starts under the little finger so the early years of youth will be represented by the period before the line touches the first horizontal line. The middle years will be represented by the space between the two horizontal lines and the latter years of life by the rest of the line.

Events can be timed on all the lines by division into three sections or a closer look can be given by reference to the figure on the facing page.

CHAPTER EIGHT

ALL ABOUT RELATIONSHIPS

A little more about this interesting subject.

The little horizontal lines which start on the side of the hand under the little finger are known as 'attachment lines' and give lots of information to the discerning hand reader.

Sadly it is seldom that one's eyes are gladdened by the deep, strongly-built, single attachment line without afflictions. For this shows on the hand of someone who will enjoy a long and happy marriage. Here marriage is taken to be for life and for richer or poorer till death do us part. (See (A) on the following diagram.)

Another, more familiar, pattern is that of two fairly strong lines. This will indicate two marriages or two strong emotional attachments. Nowadays it is not so easy to predict marriage, but as the lines show the emotion which goes into the relationship, it will be true to say that there will be two strong attachments, which under ordinary conditions would lead to marriage (B).

Where you find three or more lines you'll understand that this person finds it very difficult to stay with one

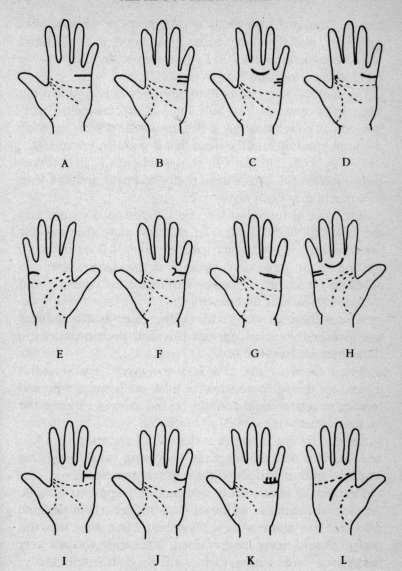

Fig 23 The Attachment Lines

person. The girdle of Venus which shows restlessness and sensitivity, also the desire to be understood, is often found with these multiple lines and you can truly say that a stable relationship is difficult for this person (C).

Upon examining one of these lines you may find that the line curves upwards. This tells a tale of success for the partner, and is particularly good if there is also a nice cross on the Jupiter mount and the heart line is good and clear (D).

The opposite situation to this is where the line curves down at the end. This shows disappointment and can lead to separation or even divorce (E).

If the line is forked at the end the person does not find the relationship fulfilling. The marriage may continue for many years, but with each partner going his or her own way more and more until, perhaps as the children come to adulthood, there is no longer any reason to continue and the partners sue for divorce (F).

Where there is an island on the line, it is a time of trouble for the marriage, but this will disappear as the difficulties are resolved (G).

Where there are two little lines together, the woman has a need for a little more stimulus than just being a wife and mother. A job or hobby could be the answer to keep the marriage going (H).

An 'ending line' appears at the end of an attachment line and signifies that the marriage is coming to an end. This might be said to actually 'cut' the attachment line (I).

The 'sign of widowhood' does not only apply to women, for men also can be widowed — witness a client of mine who has lost three wives. Maybe this is a sign that the person should never have married. It certainly was not very lucky for the wives, who all died unexpectedly. Traditionally, this line is sometimes known as the spinster line (J).

Child Lines

These are closely linked with the attachment lines. They are fine upright lines and usually stand above the attachment lines. It is said that if they cut the attachment line then the person on whom this indication is found (usually the mother) will care more for the child or children than the partner, which will not unnaturally work against the happiness of the marriage. Sometimes several lines are shown and this always indicates that the person is really fond of children and may well work with them in some capacity. Alternatively, where there are many child lines, the person may never have children of his own but will enjoy very much the company of his nephews and nieces and have a very close relationship with them. In this case, where many fine lines exist, if you look closely with a magnifying glass you will see that these do not touch the attachment lines but are situated well above them. For there to be children the child lines must *just touch*, not *cut* the attachment lines. The deeper lines are traditionally considered to be males, the finer ones to be females. Another interpretation considers that the love and care put into looking after and bringing up the child will be marked by the deeper lines. Where the lines are fine, there will be little or no time given to bringing up the children, probably because the mother's interest is elsewhere, such as in her career (K).

Broken Child Lines

This always indicates some problem with the child, either because there are difficulties in communication between parent and child or because there are physical or mental problems to be overcome. Where there is loss of a child, the line is often cut. An island on the child line shows temporary difficulties which will go away, as does the island once these are overcome (L).

Naturally it is the whole of you that is involved in a relationship, but there are of course certain sides that are more important than others and these have largely been covered earlier on. However, as the heart line deals not only with our physical heart, but also with the condition of our romantic and emotional life, we might say a few words here on the different heart lines. (See illustration p. 59)

The heart line which goes straight across the hand belongs to someone who is very controlled emotionally.

The short heart line which stops under the middle finger belongs to someone who is introverted and not too romantically or socially inclined.

The heart line which curls up towards the Jupiter finger gives the signal that this is someone who wants to relate, someone warmhearted and affectionate, above all outward-going.

Another factor which affects our relationships is, of course, the life line. Where it spreads out into the hand and so gives a full mount of Venus there is again a fund of energy and shows ambition and the ability to give love and affection.

Where the life line lies much closer to the thumb you have a much cooler character, not so expansive and with less energy. There will be a need for conservation, limitation.

If there is a girdle of Venus, showing great sensitivity and the desire for the perfect mate, you are dealing with someone who looks for perfection, a sort of knight in shining armour, not of this world, but living only in the person's imagination.

So How Can You Gauge Your Future, Lovewise?

First of all look at the influence lines.

If an influence line comes from under the heart line and joins it you may well be in line for a supportive friendship or a good business partnership (A).

Then there are influence lines which come from what is called the 'family ring' encircling the thumb and so inside the life line. These are often called worry lines as they are problems and traumas relating to the family, who may well be interfering in your love life. These are generally to be seen in the first 35 years of life (B).

Other influence lines are fine lines running alongside the life line on the mount of Venus. These represent strong friendships which mean a lot to the person. Here important people come in and out of the subject's life (C).

Remember when you are looking to predict your life ahead you must look at the time chart on p. 68. This will allow you to gauge what you have already achieved and what lies ahead of you. Another road to predicting who is coming into your life is easy to see. In (E) you see an influence line entering the fate line at approximately age 22. If after the arrival of this someone, the fate line develops an island or a crossbar then there are problems in the relationship.

Take another influence line, (D), and you will see someone arriving on the scene, but there is grave difficulty. First of all, a crossing bar showing family opposition and then an island showing doubt and uncertainty. However, you can see things improve and the line reaches the fate line, thus giving stability to the relationship, maybe marriage, and if the fate line strengthens then all will be well for the future.

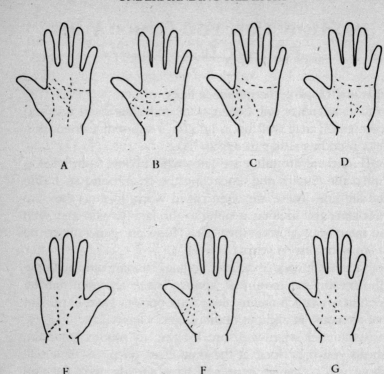

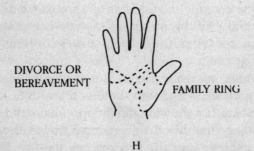

Fig 24 Influence Lines

For a relationship to become a marriage or an enduring partnership, the influence line must reach the fate line. In the next illustration, (F), we see the influence line never reaches the fate line. This shows tremendously trying delays and lack of firm conviction leading to commitment. The relationship never stabilizes and becomes a real union.

In the next illustration, (G), you see a really disastrous disappointment; the influence line cuts through the fate line. The relationship never stabilizes so there is no marriage. Always remember to gauge the effect of the marriage on the subject's life (yours, if you are checking your own), by looking at the condition of the fate line after the influence line enters the subject's life.

We mentioned earlier the little lines that follow the life line inside the Venus mount. If they continue to follow the life line all is well with the relationship, but if they start to veer off towards the thumb the marriage is failing (F).

The family ring encircling the thumb has much to do with the family fortunes and also often symbolizes marriage. Breaks in the family ring can signify divorce or separation. This can of course be checked with other indications such as the dipping down of the attachment line on the percussion to signify divorce or widowhood. The percussion is the pad of flesh at the side of the palm opposite the mount of Venus. This side of the hand under the little finger is known as the percussion as it is the side we bang the table or drum with.

It is very exciting to be able to look ahead to see your romantic future, no matter what you want out of life, for one thing is certain, we all need and look for love.

So, in checking all the items relating to love and romance in the hands remember you are reading for the whole person, so relax and allow your own intuitions and perceptions to guide you as well as the traditional indications mentioned here.

When you are looking for compatibilities where friends or members of the family are concerned, look of course to the basic hand shape, for this will tell you about the whole person. The heart line will give you a quick report of how a person responds and reacts emotionally. In the family then, where heart lines are similar the family members will share and understand their feelings, and be able to sympathize easily with one another. This is very important between a mother and her child, also between father and child, as this will aid and assist in understanding the child's need where its upbringing is concerned.

Where dealing with colleagues and friends, then the head line compatibility can be a good pointer, for its course shows similar ways of looking at things, similar likes and dislikes, an intellectual understanding. Where head lines are similar in family members, you will find they share hobbies and interests.

So those of you who are anxious to know about your future luck in love, try and follow the time chart, matching it to your own hand, and then pick out the indications ahead. If you can, do not base your findings on one factor alone, but check other areas to make sure of your verdict.

May you find great interest and excitement in doing this and of course you'll be happier still when your findings and your dreams come true.

Hand reading is such a wonderful study, you never come to the end of your learning and discoveries.

And so to recap, marriage and children.

Marriage and Children

In a hand which shows some of the markings given for success in love, marriage or deep affections are shown by a little line (or lines) that start on the side of the hand just below the little finger. These can be long, showing a long marriage, or very short.

Little light lines can be taken as romances, short affairs where the affections are captured, but not held.

Deep lines indicate serious attachments, usually marriage. Where there are two or more lines, the lower they are the earlier they occur in life. The midpoint, between the base of the little finger and the headline, is about 37 years of age. One very close to the base of the little finger would indicate marriage very late in life.

Children are marked as little lines which run down into the marriage line. Often these lines will be found in the hands of those who have not married or have not had children, but it will always be found that these people love children and have much to do with other people's children.

Assessing Your Marriage Prospects

A long and happy marriage is shown by a long, clear, well-cut line.

A number of little lines show many romances, but little likelihood of marriage.

A marriage line beginning with a fork shown on the side of the palm shows a long courtship before marriage takes place.

A fork marked at the end of the marriage line shows that the partners go their own way. They are *separated* in interest if not in fact.

A vertical line crossing the marriage line at the *end* shows the end of the marriage either through divorce or death.

A small line running very close to the marriage line either

below or above it shows either an affair just before marriage or one during the duration of the marriage.

A break in a marriage line which later continues shows a break in the marriage, a period of separation, but that the two people will come together again.

If the hand you are reading has none of the markings as given for success in love, then even if there are attachment lines under the little finger, you should be very wary in forecasting marriage, for some people are solitary by nature, and the confirmed bachelor or bachelor girl often prefers freedom and independence to the marriage tie. In order to know this you have to be able to assess the general warmth and 'outgoingness' of the hand in conjunction with the presence of the marriage lines.

Suggestions As to Picking Your Partner If You Are a Man

We can take an enjoyable trip observing and at the same time using our intuition to assess a lover, friend or prospective partner, and this first of all from a man's point of view.

'Never marry a woman with a square hand or she'll rule your life' is a quotation from the great palmist, Comte de Saint-Germain, who wrote his greatest work, *Palmistry for Professional Purposes* in 1897.

If picking a partner by the hand shape was important then, it is still important now. As society becomes more complex so do the people who live in it. For instance, a woman with a square palm today is far more of an asset from the point of view of being practical, hard-working and able to manage, because women today will not stand for being just a decoration, and most women work anyway.

Therefore, unless you have pots of money, marry a woman with square hands.

The advantage of knowing your handshapes (as shown on p.16) means you can read across the room at a party, when being introduced (the handshake is important), and when the other person isn't looking.

There is an intuitive aspect to hand reading which you can learn in five minutes, and which is very good for quick personality assessments.

If you see hands that are thin, drooping and pale, for instance, then you have a withdrawn, quiet personality that is rather passive and lacking in energy. Remember this type needs a lot of support and attention. If you have the time and a very caring nature, this one is for you, perhaps.

This system is accurate even though it is purely intuitive, because this is based on the first impression of the hand. After comparing a few hands you will see that there is as much expression shown in the hands as there is in the face, in fact more so, for, while people may control their expressions or put on an act, the movement of their hands always gives them away.

It is easy to spot the nervous, edgy, types whose fingers are always on the move, or the emotional Latin lovers who speak with their hands and often move them about quite dangerously!

The full, plump, pink hands, with fine skin, pink colour and graceful fingers belong to the real beauties of the world, the sort that model nail varnish. These women don't mind being decorative, but tend to organize other people quite readily. And although they don't mind being show-pieces (essentially for a career man) they can turn out to be quite expensive.

If the hands are perfect, their owner can be unbelievably lazy. The organizing of other people really goes along the lines of a bit of manipulation such as, 'Darling, bring me that,' or 'Would you please pass me this.' If this isn't enough and you are still keen on perfection, remember this lady is not half as soft as she makes herself out to be and can react quite forcibly when necessary, especially if the hand has any firmness to it and the fingers are long.

If you like a bit of temperament in a woman and enormous energy, look for fingernails which don't seem to reach the end of the finger and where the flesh at the finger tip looks quite prominent. It gives the fingers a squared look and the tip looks slightly snub-nosed. With this woman keep only cheap crockery in the house as it may need frequent replacement. This is not a bad type at all, it is just that her emotions are strong and earthy and she can be as affectionate as offensive. With a masculine sort of hand, these women will be hardworking, will show their emotions easily and freely, but will be extremely protective.

As thumbs are such an important part of the human hand, they play a dominant role in judging a prospective partner, lover or friend. Small thumbs on a small hand are not desirable as they indicate a person who is easily led and quite often lacks control. A very long thumb will show a person who is too dominating and in full control of her life and therefore will only be persuaded when she wants to be.

If the tip of the thumb is fine, you have someone you can impress. She is open to flattery and so you can do just this to your heart's content. She will love every minute of it. She is well aware it is all 'flannel' but nevertheless will enjoy it.

A square tip on the thumb shows that this time it won't work, and here flattery gets you nowhere. Unless she takes a liking to you in the first place, the only way round this person is with sincerity. She is not the sort you can hurry either, so take your time and be patient, allow things to take their own course.

If the thumbs are stiff, some measure of formality will be required and if you make a mistake, it may be the only one you'll be allowed to make. Not so if the thumb is supple and bends back at the first joint. If the thumb bends back at the tip these people are easy-going, tend to make the rules as they go along, and are talkative and sociable. They love to spend money. They are kind and tend to forgive and forget quite often, but never push your luck with these types as they have a nasty way of getting back at you while you're still wondering how to express your apologies. They are friendly people at heart, and if you are an unconventional type yourself, these are the partners for you, as they can adapt easily.

On the subject of flexibility, flexibility of the hand (back bending joints) is essential, and with a soft hand even better. If the fingers bend back from the palm together (when pushed of course), the person can make a home anywhere and fit into almost any environment. If you are a family type and like everything just so, whether you live in a palace or an ordinary home, this type will fall in with your ideas and adapt entirely to your way of life.

Back to the thumbs. The owner of a long, thin thumb is a studious type, and she will be quite happy curled up with an interesting bok. She likes a quiet life and will do much to achieve and keep a peaceful life style.

But if the first joint is thick and knotty you have someone who is quiet on the surface but can be quite difficult and stubborn underneath at times. These people are very perceptive and can see right through you. In fact, while she is gazing into your eyes she is probably taking you apart and putting you back together again. If the fingers are knotty at the joints as well, it's not imagination, it's really happening.

Be rather careful with the woman who holds her thumb close to the palm when the hand is relaxed. You won't find it too easy to get through to her, but you may be a bit surprised when you finally do. This type is not noted for generosity and you'll find she prefers to take rather than give. These people have one particular advantage — they can keep a secret or a confidence well.

When the thumb bends right out from the hand so that it goes at right angles to the wrist, it indicates generous, outgoing people who can keep little to themselves, especially if the tip bends back as well. These are the real chatterboxes, and if you are the sort who doesn't talk much, keeps away from parties as you are rather shy and can't think of anything to say, bring along this woman and she'll really get through your shyness. She's an instant cure for loneliness and depression.

Then look at the life line and the mount of Venus — they can tell you a lot. For instance, if you want to know if your partner or friend has a lot of energy, look for a large, fleshy, pad under the thumb, a well-developed mount of Venus. This also shows how sympathetic your prospect may be, how kindly and emotional. The deeper the pad, the deeper the emotions.

If you like travel, you'll need someone who would also enjoy it. If the beginning of the life line takes a good share of the palm base, half or more, then you're on. If the life line is so tight into the wrist that the pad is small and the line tucks under itself towards the thumb, there is not such a good resilience in the constitution for overcoming illness. This marks out the home-lover who'll only travel from necessity, or possibly even an agoraphobic.

A small thumb with a good mount of Venus would

emphasize the desire for physical, outdoor exercise and activities, not to mention some of the indoor ones. With a long thumb, of course, such a person would be hard to keep up with and might take the lead more often than you would like.

If the mount of Venus is flat, baggy, or stringy looking, there isn't much energy at all and this is reflected in the amount of warmth and sympathy this person shows. Therefore she needs a lot, and the only way to hold such a partner is to give it. If, however, you like a lot of sympathy and affection yourself, this is not the one for you.

Have you noticed how like goes to like? We are drawn to those who share our background, ideas and sympathies. Artistic types tend to link with artistic types. Basically, here we are talking about people who possess active imaginations and often high anxiety levels. It's useless being married or closely connected with someone who laughs at your worries and fears and preferable to have someone who understands.

Now if we look at the wrist where the palm begins, we have the mount of Venus on one side and the mount of Luna on the other, the percussion side.

If you hold your hand up in front of you, you can see whether both mounts are level at the base. If the base of the palm is level, this is fine. Your responses are good and well-balanced. If the mount of Luna is slightly higher than the mount of Venus then you need a lot more stimulus in your life than the average person and may find it in driving fast, in gambling, or in hard liquor.

If the mount of Luna drops down into the wrist and is lower than the mount of Venus you have a terrific imagination and will anticipate danger, you may even be frightened of the dark or of what's around the corner. In any case you need less stimulus in your life rather than more, as your already produce enough yourself to heighten your anxiety level. This excess of imagination can be used creatively in poetry or musical creation if the hand is long and narrow. If the side of the hand curves outward (bulges) then there is a desire to be original and to create, whereas if the edge is straight, interpretation of other people's ideas is the real talent, in music, language and communications generally.

If you are looking for a woman with a strong personality, it is a good idea to look for a strong first finger — one that looks a bit longer than the third finger — as this is the finger people poke you in the ribs with sometimes, or shake at you to emphasize a point. These people are often clever and most certainly sure of themselves and know what they are good at. Their organizing ability is good, so if you are a slow thinker they can make up your mind for you double quick.

An important question to ask is, how serious is this person? The finger of Saturn (the middle one) gives you this answer. If it looks very long compared to the other fingers, then you may well have a very moody type on your hands and one who will take a very serious attitude to life in general. Of course there will be advantages — she will be careful with money, plan ahead and build for the future — but be careful if the fingers are thick for she may even become miserly and you'd end up with lots in the bank and holes in your socks. Generally speaking, these people are cautious and rather pessimistic, but if you are the sort of chap who needs someone to organize your affairs, particularly the money ones, and if you don't hanker after the pub or the bright lights then this one could be right for you.

Of course if you do like to go out and play fast and loose with your hard-earned cash, then pick a woman with a short Saturn finger. They can be quite frivolous, are popular at parties and are generally good socially. This is because to them nothing is of very great importance. One thing, they never seem to be short of a few bob as they always know where to get it. As a matter of interest, people with middle fingers as long as the Apollo (third) finger were always considered to be good pickpockets — and still are, as the art of dipping depends on the scissor action of these two fingers sliding into people's pockets and gently coaxing out the wallet. These fingers being of equal length is always considered a particular asset for this profession ... Anyway, if the happy-go-lucky type is for you then look for a woman with a short Saturn finger.

The ring finger is a very important finger to look at in relation to character — after all, this is the finger you will eventually put the ring on, so it's worthwhile finding out now what the finger is like before you start decorating it. Does she already wear a ring on this finger? On the right hand is a sign of availability, because the right hand is the outgoing side of the personality. The left hand is more meaningful, for it symbolizes the inner self and the feelings. A ring on this finger — apart from meaning she's already spoken for — indicates that there are partners available and she's well aware of this fact.

A long Apollo finger is a good indication of emotional response. These people tend to take chances just to see what will happen. This is one of the signs of an adventurous spirit. If the ring finger stands away from the middle finger when the hand is at rest, so that there is wide gap, they are genuinely way out! They are really unconventional, even eccentric. They refuse to dress like drop outs to show that they are drop outs, because this is only another way of conforming. But they are drop outs pure and simple and whatever other people are doing, they do something else. So if you are looking for the unpredictable and clearly unconventional, then try this one.

If the Apollo finger lies close to the Saturn finger you have someone who is cooperative, as she does not like doing things on her own and her life will not be lived for kicks. To be emotionally satisfied she needs a partner she feels is worthwhile. These people are loyal and reliable.

The Mercury (fourth) finger is a very peculiar finger; it sits at the edge of the hand and seems to mind its own business. The side of the hand indicates the unconscious nature and just as the mount of Luna shows the imagination, our instincts and fears, so the little finger shows our unconscious activities. To some degree it is an indication of sex drive and of a talent for persuasiveness. It is is not surprising the finger is important when we consider the number of activities which it symbolizes. It has to do with our attitudes to sex and life and our business capabilities as well as our love of family and our determination, or the lack of it.

The little finger that curls itself under the others is a mark of prudishness. Spaced too far away from the others it is a mark of independence of action, a partner who would not want to be tied to the home. If the tip is sharp it suggests a quick tongue and the ability to be sarcastic. A long finger shows the ability to manipulate others. The crooked finger suggests dishonesty. If the finger is low-set, then there is a dislike of too much responsibility and a feeling of inferiority which is set into the unconscious and may be compensated for by a long first finger.

Would you like to know if this prospective partner is sexy? The answer is that this is shown by a long little finger with a fine tip, a knotty second joint and a plump third joint, next to the palm. If the Mercury finger leans gently towards the Apollo finger, you have someone who has a bit of a genius in the handling of money — in any case she will never be without.

If the second joint of the finger is bent inwards towards the palm, the joint is locked and cannot be straightened. Such a pronounced kink in the finger often indicates a woman who has painful periods and difficulty in childbirth. This is generally a hereditary complaint and to be found on other female relatives in the family.

Suggestions As To Picking Your Partner If You Are a Woman

Obviously, whether you are man or woman, the choice of a partner or even a close friend is important and it can be an especially serious business for a woman. In the past at least, little girls' ambitions seemed to be built around the sort of husband they would choose when grown up. The sort of social class they would have, the house, the country they would live in and so on all hinged on the chap they would eventually marry and so provided the subject of early fantasies and dreams. Women's lib may have changed all that.

Yet it is still more important for a woman to make the right choice than it is for a man, because for a woman the change can be very dramatic and total, even to a change of name (an interesting point for numerologists). A woman tends to be the driving force behind a man; if she is ambitious she will spur him on to achieve bigger and better things. If she likes him cuddly, she will feed him up, and if she wants him to last a long time she'll see he has time to relax and enjoy himself too. But choosing the raw material to begin with is as important as what happens afterwards. So now let's look at a few examples.

The first glance at a man's hands will show whether he digs ditches, works in an office, or doesn't have to work at all. We're back to our intuitive hand reading, where observation and intuition rule. If a man's hands are large and coarse in texture, you have a hard worker on your hands. If the thumbs are long, he can run his own business, so there need be no shortage of cash.

If the fingers are heavy and square at the tips your partner will be pedantic and orthodox, traditionally-minded, will have a love of order, discipline and routine. No way is he a 'get rich quick merchant', he is protective, plans for the future and has all the old-fashioned qualities that may sound dull, but which make for a stable and lasting marriage. If this type interests you, be sure he has a well-formed and clear fate line. (See p. 62 for the fate line.)

If the thumb is on the short side, and perhaps the fingers too, he will be even more in favour of physical activity, but less inclined to plan ahead, so you will find you have to manage the money affairs. If the thumb is on the weak side, do be sure you get your hands on the cash first, because if the second joint of the thumb has a waist and the finger tips aren't heavy squares, you might find your impetuous old devil of a husband has got through the lot on the way home. At least life won't be dull.

Back to our intuitive hand reading, and if this large, masculine hand is on the coarse side with the fingers tending to curl in and the thumbs always held close to the hand, give him a miss as it will turn out he is pretty tight-fisted. You can often tell this as this type doesn't talk much either. Such people can be tight-fisted with everything in fact. They can be very attractive though, with their air of mystery, but as they don't come across much, their charm is largely in your imagination. So forget the features for a moment, drag your eyes away and let's return to the hand reading. There are quite a few of these types about and for some strange reason women are attracted to them, but often have a rude awakening.

A nice smile is all right, but with a cold, clammy handshake it's not for you. Coldness equals selfishness, and with the clamminess there may be some physical disorder. In fact, anything which appears abnormal about the hand may simply reflect the abnormality of the personality. For example, it is natural to have moons on the nails. Those little whitish circles at the base of the nail are moons, did you say the boyfriend hasn't got any? A sure sign he's not domesticated. Don't run away with the idea you'll change all that. Because when he vanishes out of the door without a word, you may find there's the soul of a gypsy in him. These people may well marry, but its often later than the average male, and when they are married their house can be a convenience rather than a home They can be really good salesmen, but if you don't want a husband travelling in ladies' underwear, keep away.

What you should look for in a hand basically is what you look for in the rest of the man — good proportions. Have a little practice looking at people standing at bus queues and on the underground. This will train your eyes as to what the ideal looks like.

You want a hand neither too fat nor too thin (the former is sensual, the latter ascetic), but padded with solid flesh and neither too hard nor too soft to touch.

If you are a career woman who works with her head rather than her hands, the leaner sort of hands might appeal to you in a partner. Just as the ideal for a physical type of woman would be the more physical hands in a man, so the personal ideals you are looking for require you to shop around a little and find what you like.

Your man should be able to express himself emotionally;

if the stiff ones can't, it stands to reason the supple ones can. Hence the reputation of the southern European men who virtually talk with their hands and can't express much with their hands stuck in their pockets.

If the hands are tiny with fine skin, slim fingers and pointed thumbs, he may well sweep you off your feet. He's got more chat than you'd ever believe possible. Too much in fact, and there's no need to believe any of it, because these people are all talk and no do.

If they are small in stature with dark hair, they can be the super salesmen of this world, and with a well-formed little finger (that is the one they'll twist you round), they will tell you everything you want to know, and they have so much skill, flattery gets them everywhere.

Women tend to fall in love with their doctors. You can learn a lot from looking at your doctor's hands. Usually, they are a good size, very capable-looking, with heavy fingers and well-formed nails. That is the sort to look for.

A long Mercury finger on these hands shows cleverness, skill, sexual prowess, a good sense of the value of money and all sorts of natural talents.

If the little finger is too thin, your man is too ascetic, it has to be the right time and place. If the little finger is too podgy, especially with a ring, this man likes his pleasures too much, he is indolent and selfish. He likes his drink and his cigars and is not too fond of work.

If you like the sporting type, hair on the back of the hand isn't necessary but it's a start, because it confirms he's a sporting type and definitely an out-of-doors character, especially with a large mount of Venus. Sometimes the hair is only on the back of the hand behind the little finger. It is quite difficult to get these types out of the bedroom. If the hair is on the right hand behind the little finger, try waving a fiver under his nose — it usually stirs his enthusiasm. The little finger is a good indication of a man's ability to communicate with others.

The left hand being the more intimate side of life and the right hand the business activities, a ring on the little finger gives a man away every time. The ring on the right little finger will show it's money he is after and the ring on the left little finger shows it's sex which is more important to him.

You may like a man who has more *savoir faire* and refinement. If so, you need a hand which is not so broad and therefore less materialistic, a hand that looks longish because of this, but has square tips to the fingers, a hand with a fine skin texture and a good colour, not the pale, wishy-washy, lifeless-looking hand of the man who does nothing unless he has to do it. You want to see a good healthy pink that glows with vitality, and a good firmness to the grip. You expect the fingers to be slimmer and the thumb as well, but these digits should not be too thin, bony and dried up. They should be expressive in their mobility, but without the agitation of the Latin types.

If the skin is so fine at the back of the hand that the veins can be seen, and these stand up slightly, then you have an academic quality — refinement plus maturity. The fingernails in this case should be slightly oblong, otherwise the emotional depths may be lacking. If there is over-refinement and boniness to these hands, then you have the old-fashioned aristocrat — the snappy dresser who is over-particular about his food, hygiene, and so and so forth. They can be too finicky for words. Unless you are finicky too, don't bother. They can make your life a misery.

While we are on the subject of fingernails, it is worth noting that a long narrow nail that comes to a point at the palm end is not a strong type of nail by any means. Conversely, if the nail is very short and broad, broader than it is long in fact, you have the critic who will argue for the sake of arguing and who also has a quick temper. These people will give you a dog's life unless you are a really tough person who can find other uses for a frying pan. After all, it is the women who are supposed to have the monopoly on nagging!

If you find this sort of nail on a broad hand that is short in length and thick with nobbly joints on the fingers and thick thumbs, you are looking at a sadistic type of character who has served his apprenticeship as a nasty little boy, grew up to be a Billy Bloggs and went through a phase of quite enjoying nipping and pinching people. You won't see many of these hands about, but once you've seen them, you won't forget what they look like — or feel like for that matter.

If you like conversation, try a man whose thumbs bend back at the tips; he'll talk about anything, and he's sociable and will probably spend his last penny on you.

Of course if you want sensible conversation, try the one whose first finger is longer than his ring finger, but make sure the tip is nicely rounded or tapered. This one can discuss for hours and is probably a schoolteacher anyway. Of course he can be on the dry side, so far as conversation is concerned, but really dry conversation comes from the chap with the very long middle finger, especially when it looks thin and knotty at the joints. This type makes a good analyst. The trouble is, he's probably analysing you! As a career these types like the sciences, and analytical chemistry is the sort of thing that turns them on.

Now take a nice long ring finger, a little longer than the first finger — these types have a slightly warmer, more personal conversation. If this finger is very long, nearly as long as the middle finger, they may be a little scatterbrained, but they are warm, human, like to get along with people on the personal level, and they like nothing better than a garden fence to lean on — this is the ideal speaking platform for them. A little finger, of course, prefers the front parlour, but you'll have understood that from the above.

If you like a man to do things around the home (and what woman doesn't), there are two sorts to choose from. One is the spatulate type of hand. Perfect ones, where the wrist end of the hand is narrow and seems to broaden out as it spreads towards the fingers, are rarely seen. The most common form is simply the spatulate tips to the fingers. The flesh at the nail tip is spatulate and the tips seem to fan out slightly.

If the spatulate tip is on the ring finger, the man concerned will favour a bit of cooking. If the spatulate tip is on the middle finger, decorating is his forte, but generally, if all the tips have spatulate ends, he will even have a bash at repairing the television. These types are curious and ingenious, like to find out how things work and can even turn their hand to inventing them. One thing is certain: this man has lots of energy. He will be restless and always fishing around for something to do, so if you want to keep him out of the neighbours' house/garage/allotment, make sure there's plenty to fix around your own home, otherwise he may wander.

The other sort who likes pottering around the house is the owner of the more effeminate type of hand. Now this one you will have to watch, for he's inclined to set up in competition. It stands to reason that if his hands are more beautiful, i.e. effeminate, than yours, he's putting you out of a job. Don't underrate this type — such a man can be fantastic at flower arranging, planning, interior decorating and dressmaking and can even do your hair. It doesn't follow he's less of a man because of this.

Fundamentally, these people's sense of appreciation, evaluation and taste is high. They can usually spot originals from copies, play the piano beautifully and have expansive and cultured personalities.

The Venus mount tends to show the ambitious qualities in a man. For vitality it must be full, for it protects the underlying artery. Without this vitality your ambitious man is a dreamer. The life line encircling the Venus mount must be well-defined to show determination, and sweep well into the palm to show expansiveness and generosity. If it is straight with the top end rather high going to the mount of Jupiter under the first finger, he's a bit of an egotist, but he'll make his way in the world. Sweeping out past the middle of the wrist indicates a strong constitution, good recovery from illness and an out-of-doors type who likes to travel and is likely to live a long time.

With a well-developed mount of Luna your man has good foresight and can plan ahead constructively. If the padding is thick near the wrist, fine, for he'll plan ahead for you too, and will be more inclined to wine and dine you, take you dancing and whisper romantic words in your ear. With a straight edge to the side of the hand under the little finger he can even anticipate your thoughts. If the edge of the hand curves out this shows his originality. Not only will he be enthusiastic about your ideas, he will also add some of his own to yours.

If the base of the hand is very broad yet it is very narrow across the knuckles, you have a sweet-natured man who is fond of his own physique and may be a bit of a showman. This isn't so bad as he normally has the physique to go with it, if the base of the hand is also fleshy and firm.

If the middle of the palm is broadest and well padded you have the good organizer, but one who can be stubborn and dig in his heels. Broad across the knuckles and heavy-boned from the back shows a dynamic personality with too much uncontrollable energy. In a coarse hand this will indicate anything from a boxer to a psychopath. So be a little wary about choosing this type of character.

Finally, you will want to know who is going to be boss, or wear the trousers. This one's easy: look at the palm of your hand, close your fingers together and your thumb up to the side of the palm. How far up the third phalange of Jupiter, the first finger, does your thumb reach with the hand straight? Now compare it with your boyfriend's hand — how far does his thumb reach? The winner wears the pants.

Don't worry about the length of the first finger — you'll remember this is the one you wag at people when you are threatening them. Don't worry about the little or Mercury finger — this is the one you twist people around. Just consider the thumb, because this is the one that decides the will-power and who wins in the end.

So you can see how much can be learnt by a simple examination of the hand shape, sometimes using your intuition and sometimes just ordinary common sense, which if you've lived a few years you will come to realize is not so ordinary as you might think, and is all too often sadly lacking in people's actions.

Will You Be Lucky?

Yes, there is such a thing as luck and this is shown in the hand, where you will find it if you look.

First of all you are generally lucky if you have many squares marked in your hand, for these always indicate providential protection and a sort of charmed life.

There is a marking in the hand called the 'angle of luck' and this is formed by the space between the end of the head line and the end of the life line. The wider the space

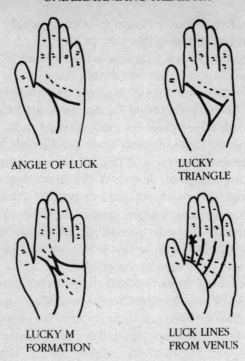

ANGLE OF LUCK

LUCKY
TRIANGLE

LUCKY M
FORMATION

LUCK LINES
FROM VENUS

Fig 25 Luck Lines

between them, the luckier you are. Sometimes you see a narrow space on the person's left hand and a much wider one on the right hand and you can conclude that the person has greatly increased his luck by his own efforts.

Another lucky sign to have is called the 'lucky triangle' and is formed by the lines of life, head and health. Since is is similar to the angle of luck, again the wider the extent of the triangle, the greater the luck.

If you look carefully at the palm of the hand you will sometimes be able to discern what is called the 'lucky M formation'. This is shaped by the line of fate crossing the lines of head and heart and so forming the capital letter M.

This has been traditionally taken as a sign of money/marriage and good fortune in love.

Signs of money luck are shown in the hand by certain lines rising from the mount of Venus.

A line running upwards from the mount of Venus to the mount of Jupiter under the first finger is a good omen. It is a forecast of advancement, promotion, authority and financial success. Lucky portents are heightened when the line ends in a star.

A line running from the mount of Venus to the base of the second or Saturn finger shows a money increase as a result of the person's own efforts and family backing.

A line running from the mount of Venus to the base of the little finger shows money from commercial or scientific pursuits.

Whoever wins the pools should have a line running from the mount of Venus to below the third or Sun finger, for this line shows windfalls.

Travel Lines

So-called travel lines really show the person's desire to travel and his restlessness. Other things being equal, i.e., if the opportunity and money are there and there are not too many responsibilities, the person will travel.

Travel lines, or lines of restlessness, are shown on the mount of the Moon, on the edge of the palm opposite the mount of Venus. Many lines, many trips, deep lines, important journeys.

When the life line forks at its base and one fork points towards the mount of the Moon, then it is likely that the person will make his home in a country other than the land of his birth.

Lines and Marks on the Palm

Some hands are clear of all but the major lines, others are criss-crossed with lines and little markings which have a significance in themselves.

In general one can say that a person with a relatively clear palm is much less nervous and sensitive than the person with many small lines and markings.

Life is an easier matter for the clear-palmed person, since he does not react strongly and is more self-contained and self-centred.

Minor markings on the hand apply to the area in which they are found and affect that area of life for good or ill.

The minor marks are stars, squares, crosses, islands, triangles, chains, breaks, tassels and forks.

The fortunate signs are squares and stars indicating protection and good luck, as does the triangle.

The adverse signs are chains, islands and circles, indicating as they do upsets, restrictions and difficulties.

A break in the line usually shows a change of direction. A break in the life, heart or head lines is adverse for health.

Tassels at the end of a line show the dispersion of force and are sometimes shown at the end of the head line. A cross shows adversity or unhappiness, and the fork is similar to the tassel in meaning.

Spiritual Development

Marks for spiritual development should be looked for in the hand for they can have an important bearing on the life and so enable you to slant your reading correctly.

These are the mystic cross and bow of intuition.

The mystic cross lies in the centre of the quadrangle between the lines of head and heart.

When present it always shows one whose life consciously or unconsciously will be much influenced by the occult. The person himself may be involved in occult and spiritual work or it may be someone closely related to him.

Another sign which is often present with the mystic cross is the ring of Solomon. This is a line that encircles the base of the index finger and runs from between the index and middle fingers to the outer edge of the palm. Traditionally it is a sign of wisdom and adepthood.

The Bow of Intuition

This is a semi-circular mark and lies in the area of the mount of the Moon. It shows exceptional intuitive and psychic ability and is practically always found on the hands of mediums, psychics and those in whom the ESP faculty is present and developed.

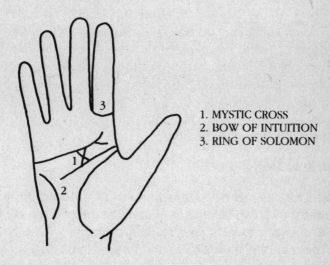

1. MYSTIC CROSS
2. BOW OF INTUITION
3. RING OF SOLOMON

Fig 26 Spiritual Development and Potentialities

The presence of these signs on the palm indicates that progress and development along higher lines is possible to the persons concerned, but whether they will always use their gifts in a positive way is entirely up to them.

CHAPTER NINE

HEALTH

There are some things which are certain in life and the need for good health to achieve happiness and success is one of them. Some people are born healthy and continue so all their lives, others have to work at it in caring for themselves by paying attention to the food they choose to eat, by exercising regularly and by avoiding any abuse of their bodies as through drinking too much, smoking or using drugs. So caring for the body in this basic sort of way at least gives it a chance to keep fit and renew its energies as required.

The hand can be an excellent indicator of both our strengths and weaknesses in the field of health. In this chapter we shall look to interpreting some of these indications as seen in the hand.

Hand Types

As we know there are certain hand types (already discussed

in Chapter Three) and each of these has its own health indications. We will look at these in turn.

The Elementary Type

This type of person is basically healthy, thrives in the open air and generally enjoys good health, apart from any accidents relating to his employment, until late in life. He has a tendency to depressive illness in later life.

The Square and Oblong Types

These are generally healthy people, but the square likes to do everything correctly and therefore tends to worry. It is this tendency to worry which leads to stress and so can later bring illness. It is wise for these folk to take regular breaks from work. Demanding hobbies are often their saviour as they have to concentrate all their energies on their hobbies and so have no time or energy to worry. The traditional seaside holiday with little to do but sit on the beach toasting themselves really does little to relax them and so is not to be recommended.

The Spatulate Type

These are the vital ones, always full of restless energy. It follows that they rarely relax for the very good reason they always have energy to spare and so need to have ways of burning it up usefully. Their general health is excellent.

The Conic Type

It is said of these people that they can dig their graves with their teeth. Towards middle life conic types tend to run to fat. The phrase 'fair, fat and forty' is an everyday saying which refers to some conic types. To keep their health and beauty the conics need to moderate their appetites and so avoid too much sugar and carbohydrates. Altering their eating habits can save them many problems.

The Psychic Type

The most sensitive and impressionable of all the types, they do not have the basic sturdy constitutions possessed by the others. They do not find coping with the real world easy and can take to the escapes provided by drink or drugs. As they are often allergic to these, their form of escape is really another form of servitude to a habit. They do better with a loving, understanding, practical partner who can handle all the daily complexities of living.

Skin
Texture/Colour/Temperature

Where the skin is very sensitive, as in the psychic type mentioned above, there is sensitivity to the environment, to airborne germs, to virus infections and really to anything that is going. Where the skin is tougher there is less sensitivity to the environment and so to germs. If the skin is dry and scaly there may be an underactive thyroid, overactive if the hands are warm and wet.

The normal skin colour on the palm of the hand is a rosy pink, showing good health and naturally good functioning of all the body systems. If the skin is red it suggests there may be a tendency to high blood pressure and one could tactfully suggest that if a recent check has not been carried out that this should be done in the normal course of caring for the health. A pale skin suggests lack of energy. This could be due to anaemia and is often found in women of child-bearing age. Some good iron mixture tablets could be the answer. Where the skin shows up as yellow then there may be liver problems such as jaundice or even a recent bilious attack. If the hands feel cold, although the room in which you are sitting is warm, then there is poor circulation.

We can see from this that there are certain signs in the hand which give an immediate and yet general indication of the health of the person whose hands are in front of you. You can note whether the hand is too soft (lack of energy, lazy perhaps!) or too hard (emotionally repressed?) The hand should feel warm to the touch and be of a nice consistency. The nails should be free of ridges, whether vertical or horizontal, a matter we will deal with later in more detail. The nails should have moons on all fingers and on the thumbs. The finger tips should not be crossed with lines. The lines on the hands should not be too criss-crossed with lines, for if so, this shows hypersensitivity. The health line should be single and unbroken. The life line and all the other major lines should be strongly defined.

Stress

We now know how much tension and stress contribute to the onset of physical illness. Everyone seems to be agreed that the ability to relax would help to reduce the stress, which causes tensions, hence the growth of new movements finding favour in this country and in the West generally — meditation, yoga and tai-chi for example — all of which aim to teach Westerners to relax.

In viewing a number of hands it will be borne in on you that there are two main types: those with the *empty* hand and those with the *full* hand. The empty hand has only the major lines — the life, head, heart and the fate line (A). The full hand has a network of lines criss-crossing the palm showing hypersensitivity (B). It is this hand which gives most evidence of stress, although with a good head line and thumb the owner will be able to overcome and cope with the various difficulties of life maybe better than the owner of the empty hand. However, we have to say that these people with the full hand are the worriers, with nervous systems which react to the least stress. The nervous system never relaxes, it is always on guard — a habit learnt in childhood probably, where the environment was hostile and the child had to be on its guard to safeguard itself. This habit is almost impossible to break in later life.

Exhaustion can be seen by the dropping in of the skin on the finger tips accompanied by downward lines, which are generally curved to fit the drooping of the skin (C). Where you see this indication do suggest the person eases up as soon as possible.

Other Stress Indicators

Where you see lines running across the fingertips (D), you can be sure there are unresolved problems relating to the fingers on whose tips you can see the lines. The more of these little horizontal lines you can see on any finger tip the deeper the problem to be resolved and the more urgent that it should be done so.

If there are many lines on the tip of the forefinger then the problem relates to the ego and self-confidence. If on the Saturn or middle finger, then the problem to be faced has to do with career or security. If on the Apollo or ring finger,

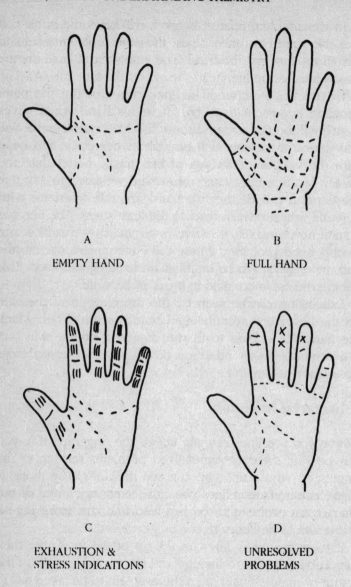

A

EMPTY HAND

B

FULL HAND

C

EXHAUSTION &
STRESS INDICATIONS

D

UNRESOLVED
PROBLEMS

Fig 27 Health Indications

then the problem relates to love, children or creativity. If the little finger has these lines, then the problem relates to sexual frustrations or difficulties, or to difficulties in literary or scientific expression.

In practice it is rarely easy to pinpoint the problem, except perhaps to find the finger with the 'mostest', as usually all the fingers will have these little cross bars. It will be necessary to look at the whole hand to see what has brought this about. Always bear in mind that character is destiny and as character can be seen in the hand, so of course can the destiny. It is possible, but not easy, to determine whether a condition of stress or actual illness is coming or going. Things start first in the positive hand (the right hand if you are right-handed), then move over to the subjective hand. When both hands are equally affected then the condition has reached its peak and should then begin to recede, first from the positive hand, then from the subjective hand. Were you to find the condition only in the right hand, generally the positive hand, you would assume that it was just starting. If only on the subjective hand (generally the left), you would assume that it was on its way out.

The Fingerprint Patterns as Health Indicators

These patterns are genetic, form the unchanging part of our character structure, and so exert a sort of basic influence on our health or tendency to contract certain diseases.

The Loop Pattern

These people have the advantage of being adaptable,

WHORL PRINT

ARCH PRINT

LOOP PRINT

TENTED ARCH

COMPOSITE
PRINT

COMPOUND
PRINT

Fig 28 Fingerprint Patterns

versatile and expressive. They can fly from one extreme to another, which makes them unpredictable and unreliable in that they can so easily change their ideas and attitudes. Healthwise, this pattern predisposes to nerve trouble, digestive weakness and faulty heart conditions. (These findings are according to the researches of Noël Jaquin and the members of the society to which he belonged.)

The Arch Pattern

These are rather serious people. They find it difficult to express their inner thoughts and feelings, so often suffer from emotional repression and psychosomatic problems. They keep everything to themselves, being both secretive and suspicious. Although this may not be an easy pattern to work with it can be improved if those who have it try their hand at some practical, creative hobby which will help them to exteriorize their feelings and ideas and so maintain good health. Physiologically, there is a predisposition to faulty digestive action.

The Whorl Pattern

These people are fixed, determined and individualistic with a tendency to unconventionality. They may maintain a traditional attitude for the most part, but they will spurn conventions when it suits them. What they feel they feel very deeply, but they do not discuss their feelings, for in all they do they are guarded and careful. They tend to be rather slow in response and are rarely adaptable. They expect you to adapt to them. Physiologically, this pattern predisposes to nervous digestive problems and faulty heart action.

The Tented Arch Pattern

Highly-strung and idealistic, these people are sensitive and emotional. They are often impulsive and find that it is hard for them to realize their ideals. Healthwise, they have a predisposition to nervous troubles. They should not have too many heavy problems to solve as they do not have the determination of the whorl-pattern type.

The Composite Pattern

Twin loops oppose each other. Mentally these people are open to two opposing views, ideas or impressions. Often they suffer from inner conflicts and self-doubt. Fortunately, they are practical so can solve their problems by practical means. They can be very critical and resentful. Healthwise, there is a predisposition to general toxic conditions.

The Compound Pattern

The most usual manifestation of this is a little whorl within a loop, although any two different patterns linked together within one fingerprint is called a compound. If the pattern is the whorl within the loop, these are practical people who combine the charm and tact of the loop with the determination and observation of the whorl. This is often called a Peacock's Eye and if found on the third fingertip it is said to protect you from all manner of dangers and evils. Healthwise, there are quite a few predispositions, such as to digestive weakness, nerve troubles and faulty heart action. Incidentally, I heard from a student that he found three subjects with this fingerprint pattern on their thumbs who proved to be dyslexic. Of course this is not enough research to prove anything conclusive, but it is interesting and might provide the basis for further investigations by someone interested.

In giving these health predispositions it must be remembered that these *are* merely predispositions and do not have to manifest if the subject looks after his health. There are many health conditions which can be seen fairly easily in the hand if you know where to look and the short list below can help to point you in the right direction in finding out what is ailing you. It cannot, of course, give you the whole answer to your problem — that's up to your physician.

Some Health Conditions

Acidity

This is mentioned here as it is the breeding ground for a very common complaint, rheumatism, and can be seen first of all in a cluster of little upright lines between the heart and head lines on the percussion (D). There is a build-up of uric acid, and if not checked then the finger joints or other parts of the body begin to ache. It is wise to cut out those things which are acid forming from the diet, including all citrus fruits.

Allergies

These come in many shapes and sizes and are due to sensitivities to different foods, drugs or drinks. A very common allergy is hayfever, where the sufferer is sensitive to pollen. Although the hand cannot point out what

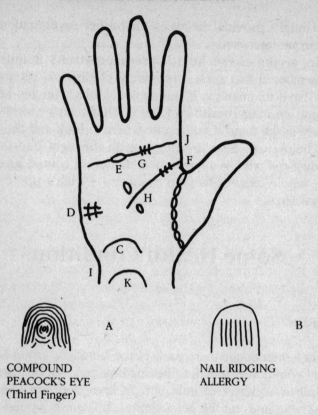

COMPOUND
PEACOCK'S EYE
(Third Finger)

A

NAIL RIDGING
ALLERGY

B

Key:

C. Allergy line
D. Tendency to rheumatic conditions
E. Eye weaknesses
F. Childhood chest problems
G. Teeth
H. Islands on health line (illness). Digestive problems
I. Gynaecological and urogenital problems
J. Migraine (clots on head line)
K. Rascette rising into palm. Childbirth difficulties

Fig 29 Health Problems

particular substance is the offending allergen, it can point out if you are someone who is at risk in this respect. There is a line which lies at the base of the Luna mount (C), technically called the Via Lascivia, and if you possess it the old palmistry taught you were a particularly lustful character with a leaning towards all sorts of depravities, which of course turned and attacked you in the shape of illnesses. Traditional readings became adapted to less black-and-white times and it is now generally agreed that if you have this line you are sensitive to various substances.

Some palmists say that allergies can be seen by vertical ridging on the nails, others state that this vertical ridging has to do with spinal injuries, or injuries to do with other bones in the body. Probably not enough research has gone into this subject. Since palmistry is only just beginning to be taken seriously by the medical profession, there is no funding of research and palmists are not rich enough to do this funding themselves since they are too busy reading hands for a living. Many people are allergic to dairy products and as there are now reliable allergy analysts available, if you are in doubt then send a sample of your hair or your handwriting (that is, comply with what the firm asks you to send), so that they can analyse your allergies. You will find this is very helpful as you can then cut down on, or cut out, those things which do not agree with you.

Eyes, Ears, Teeth

All islands on the lines of the hand show too much sodium in the diet, that is, an imbalance between sodium and potassium. In other words, you need more potassium or less sodium. Less salt and more kelp or something similar. Having said this, traditionally, we are told that an island on

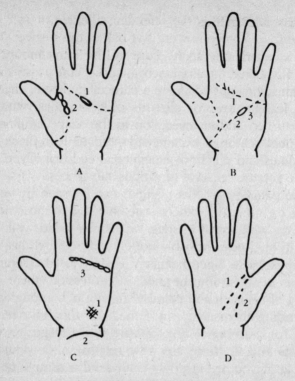

Fig 30 Health Conditions

the heart line under Apollo or the third finger (A1) shows a sight weakness and therefore anyone seeing this in their hand should go for an eyesight test. Very often if the condition is left untreated a series of small lines appear, again under the Apollo finger. An island or the chaining of the life line under the Jupiter or forefinger (A2) suggest that childhood throat problems or bronchial trouble can lead in later life to deafness.

Teeth problems and the need to go for a dental appointment can be seen by little lines above the heart line and under the Saturn or middle finger (B1).

Digestive Difficulties

These are generally seen in or around the Mercury line, which traditionally was named the 'liver line', thus exactly explaining the state of our digestion. If there are digestive difficulties they can be seen in oblique lines coming up from the life line towards the Mercury finger (B2). Sometimes islands on the Mercury line (B3) can be the sign of chest problems such as bronchitis and pneumonia. People with these signs should either give up or reduce their smoking level.

Problems Related to the Reproductive System

Any problems in this direction are generally to be found at the base of the mount of Luna. There may be lots of little lines criss-crossing there which warn of gynaecological difficulties with women and urogenital problems with men (C1). I have also noted that where the first rascette rises up into the palm (C2) women have difficulty with childbirth and it is also a sign that the family will not be large. The rascettes are also a health indicator. Smoking thins them.

Circulatory Problems

Cold hands often point to circulatory problems, that is, if the hands are cold when the temperature actually suggests they should be warm. As children these people may well have suffered with chilblains. Other indications are the colour of the nails which may be pale and maybe blue at the base, suggesting anaemia, or red, which goes to the other extreme and suggests high blood pressure, a factor which can easily be checked by a visit to your doctor. The heart line itself should not be chained. This could be due to a mineral deficiency and it should be checked. If the heart line is frayed or broken then a check-up might be advisable (C3).

Headaches

These can be seen very clearly and are marked by little dots on the head line. These little dots are also present when the much more severe form of headache is present, the migraine (D1). Clinics for this latter problem can be found — although not in abundance they are in many major cities. Apparently they do have good results if treatment is continued. A new treatment is, I believe, being tested, consisting of goggles which apparently get rid of the migraine after they have been worn for a reasonably short length of time. However, at the time of writing, January 1990, these are not yet on supply to the general public.

Backache

Backache, which is a problem from which many people suffer, can be seen in a series of dots on the life line (D2). These dots are similar to those mentioned on the head line with reference to headaches and migraine. In both cases the length of time the dots continue on the life or head lines marks the length of time the subject suffers from these problems. However, if the markings are only on the subjective (generally left) hand it shows that the problems are receding and will soon be gone.

Mineral Deficiencies

To maintain good health it is important to learn to relax and take life philosophically (easier said than done), and to try to avoid mineral and vitamin deficiencies. These can be seen mainly in white spots on the nails, which generally suggest a lack of calcium and coincide either with the individual having a cold or the 'flu.

If the nails are brittle or split easily, then biochemical remedies could well be the answer. They can be obtained from any health food store. Where the lines, the head or heart for example, are islanded or chained, then some mineral or vitamin deficiency exists. Often zinc will help the islanded or pitted head line to think less confusedly and to worry less. Alternative therapists such as homoeopaths or radionic practitioners should be able to pinpoint your mineral and vitamin deficiencies and so enable you to make a complete return to good health. In fact quite often small deficiencies can account for a disabling lack of good health and enjoyment of life, which we all want so much.

Unfortunately there are myriad other diseases or predispositions which could be listed. Such a detailed list would not be helpful here, but help can be found in the study of palmistry.

Probably the most important factor in everyone's life is keeping the health they were (in most cases) fortunate to be born with. This is easily maintained in childhood and in early adulthood unless the person begins to take liberties with his body by abusing it through taking to drink or drugs, or by deliberately taking foolish risks in fast cars or other activities which generally guarantee a short life. It is later, from the middle years onwards, that people begin to reap what they have sown and it is probable that the wise ones will change their life style and habits in order not to put so much stress on the body and so attain for themselves some measure of joy and happiness for the work that they have put in. It seems really that some philosophy of life or a strong religious instinct and interest are the best ways of keeping one's body, mind and soul in good order and getting the best out of life. The Buddhist 'Middle Way' of avoiding the extremes of the opposites seems a very civilized way of living one's life without harming others sharing this planet with us. Maybe too there will be those who can also find good health and harmony from their study of hand reading.

CHAPTER TEN

CAREER INDICATIONS IN THE HAND

Most human beings wish to succeed and for many this means fulfilment through the right career.

Making the right choice careerwise can often be helped through the interpretation of the hand shape and patterns by a skilled hand reader. We can even help ourselves if we learn to study and interpret the hand skilfully.

To some the acme of achievement will be the attainment of a degree, to others academic success will mean very little, for their talents will lead them in other directions. For those who wish to win sporting accolades, there will be a need for self-discipline and long hours of tedious practice. Any number of fields can be mentioned to show the diversity of human endeavour and to point out that happiness and success depend ultimately on the individual's aims and goals and of course on the determination with which he pursues them. So while the palmist can suggest an occupation, a person can succeed in anything, provided the will and the desire are there to do so.

For most of us the correct career choice will go a long

way towards making our lives happy and fulfilled.

We will first take a generalized look at possibilities by looking at the various hand shapes first put forward by Fred Gettings. These are simple, easy to recognize and describe and give a general indication of career choice.

These four divisions are the air, fire, earth and water hands.

The Air Hand

The palm is square, the fingers long (as long as the palm or even longer) (A). The lines are usually fine, but well-formed.

The air types above all need to communicate, to mix, to read and to understand. They have quick inquisitive minds and like to know how things work. Emotionally, they fear commitment, preferring to go through life untrammelled and uncommitted. As communication is the big thing, these people are generally suited to work in the media and allied fields.

The Fire Hand

The palm is rectangular and the fingers are short. (B) There are a large number of strong, firm lines on the fire hand.

Fire hand people are always on the go, activity is their forte, they like to get things done and to influence others to their way of thinking. They like to enjoy life and have plenty of energy, enthusiasm and go. They are leaders and extroverts, generally winners too.

The fire hand is happy in any situation where there is

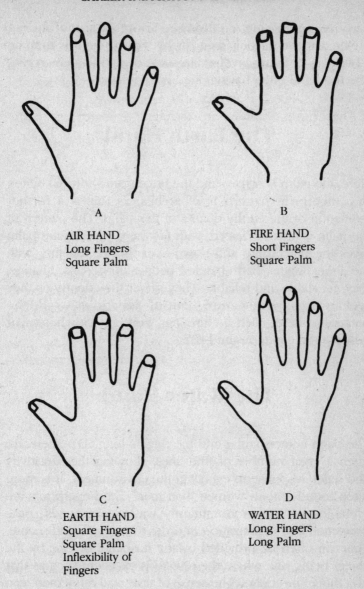

A

AIR HAND
Long Fingers
Square Palm

B

FIRE HAND
Short Fingers
Square Palm

C

EARTH HAND
Square Fingers
Square Palm
Inflexibility of
Fingers

D

WATER HAND
Long Fingers
Long Palm

Fig 31 Divisions of Hands into Air, Fire, Earth and Water

activity and some challenge. Sport is sometimes a preference even if only as a hobby. For others it is running a business or being involved in some demanding enterprise. The fire hand often has whorled fingerprints.

The Earth Hand

Here, the palm is square and the fingers are short (C). Often the fingerprint pattern is of arches, as this is a further intimation of the earthy quality of this hand. The pattern of the palm is uncomplicated, with few lines. The square palm gives the practicality and down-to-earthness, together with the short fingers. Earth-handed people do not like change, they are stable and reliable. They prefer the country as they feel in tune with nature. Out-of-door jobs would be preferable here, such as farming, working with horses or policing the commons and parks.

The Water Hand

The palm is rectangular and the fingers long (D). There are often a great number of fine lines, showing the sensitivity and quick response to events in the environment. It is more often found among women than men. The fingerprints are often loops. The predominantly water type needs some protection and organization in order to feel safe and secure. This can often be provided by the husband, or else by the career being one where the reward is excellent such as that of a model or actress. The sense of taste and refinement can lead some water types to take up these careers.

I have given these very general indications for various careers as they can act as a quick basic suggestion for the type of career which would fit in with the person's hand shape. Later on we can look in more detail at the possibilities.

Often then, palmistry enables the hand reader to suggest the right type of employment for youngsters who may not be at all sure what they want to do, and parents often bring their teenagers for help in this direction. Again, it is helpful in middle life when a person would like a change of direction, but is not sure whether the way they really want to go will make for success and fulfilment. This can be assessed by an examination of the hand. The use of palmistry for career assessment can be a great help as the correct job makes for the happy person, or at least the satisfied customer in one area of life.

The Outdoor Types

To some the great outdoors calls. We have just been looking at the earth hands and often these like some job which allows them to work out-of-doors, if not able to be in the country itself, although on the whole the country life is preferable.

We mentioned earlier on in Chapter Four that there were four different fingertips, each of which has different character indications. It is the spatulate tip which has a dislike of working indoors and so gravitates to outside jobs. There are many of these, skilled and unskilled.

Forestry, agriculture, horticulture and farming, building and various construction jobs make for a great variety of opportunities in this field. Then there is transport — long distance lorry-drivers, for example. Then you have people like postmen, milkmen and other delivery types. All our commons and parks require people to look after them. There are opportunities there for gardeners and wardens.

Other work opportunities attractive to those who prefer the out-of-doors are to do with sport — golf, rugby, tennis or cricket for example.

In considering the attraction to working in the open air we can also include those who would like to go to sea. These people have a good development of the Luna mount and a strong Venus mount sweeping out into the hand as well (*See* p. 35.)

Business Types

The main indication for success in this field is to possess a full set of fine square tips to the fingers. This gives a logical, practical, methodical type of mind necessary to business life. There are many fields open to this type according to his skill and intelligence. These are along clerical lines, which are very remunerative in some cases, such as accountancy, banking, computer work and bookkeeping. The square tips bestow a mind which likes to do everything accurately, neatly, and with professionalism. Probably all the personal possessions such as diaries and home files will also be as neatly arranged as the columns of figures at work.

The tried and tested ways are often thought to be best and the usual businessperson is not all that flexible either in his habits or in his ideas and so not so easy to get along with in a personal sense.

There is a skin ridge pattern which is common to those people in business or the professions and this is the 'loop of

CAREER INDICATIONS IN THE HAND

OUTDOOR TYPE

A. SPATULATE FINGERTIPS
B. BROAD VENUS
C. DEEP LUNA FOR SEAFARING
D. AFFINITY WITH NATURE

BUSINESS TYPE

A. LONG JUPITER FINGER
B. LOOP OF EXECUTIVE ABILITY
C. LOOP OF SERIOUS INTENT
D. LONG STRAIGHT HEAD LINE
E. FATE LINE

LEADER, ADMINISTRATOR

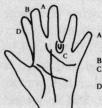

A. GAP BETWEEN FIRST & SECOND FINGERS
B. OUTWARD TURN
C. LOOP OF SERIOUS INTENT
D. SHORTER JUPITER FOR SELF-EMPLOYMENT OR SALES

MANUAL WORKER

A. ARCH FINGERPRINT
B. WHORL FINGERPRINT

ENTERTAINMENT, AND WORK WITH THE PUBLIC

A. FATE LINE FROM LUNA
B. LONG THIRD FINGER WHORL IN TIP FOR CREATIVITY
C. MUSICAL TALENT
D. SUN LINE
E. WRITER'S FORK

TEACHING & THE MEDICAL WORLD

A. MEDICAL STIGMATA
B. LONG LITTLE FINGER
C. LONG HEAD LINE
D. TEACHER'S SQUARE

Fig 32 Career Indications

serious intent'. This really does state exactly the character-istic held by those people who are lucky enough to possess it. These people take life seriously and wish to get ahead. They do not wish to waste their time and so, in most cases, get ahead in their chosen profession.

Another indication for a business career would be a straight head line. The owners of these have an eye for opportunity and a good business sense. A long, straight fate line used to be the indication of a successful business career. It may be, but it will also be a long plod, perhaps reflecting someone who stays in the same job for a lifetime.

As all the lines show our psychological attitudes and the fate line especially indicates the person's attitude to career matters, it does not always follow that the owner of a long fate line from the base of the hand up to the Saturn (middle) finger will stay in the same job. Outside circumstances may interfere with such plans and force a probably unwelcome change. The fact is that the person with such a fate line would not like change, and so would not make a major change, once settled, from choice.

Are You a Leader? An Administrator? How About Self-Employment?

These are all under one heading as they all require ambition and self-confidence.

When you look at the hands, see whether the first and second fingers are apart and the first finger is turned slightly outward. This gives the ability to make decisions and it is one which shows initiative, a talent invaluable in running a business or any sort of organization.

The leader, as all the palmistry books which have ever been written will tell you, is the chap or lady with the long Jupiter (first) finger. They are leaders as they are full of self-confidence, completely self-assured and natural. Such people make good 'heads' and also good salespeople, for their confidence is transferred to their product. People feel this and buy.

If the person with a long first finger also has square-tipped fingertips, a loop of serious intent and a good fate line, he can reach the top as head of his company or at least among the 'top ten'.

Like everything else, the person who really is determined to get to the top of the tree and yet has not this long magic finger, but a shorter Jupiter, *can* reach the dizzy heights he seeks, but statistically less often. The Jupiter or first finger shorter than the Apollo or third finger shows a self-appreciation problem. It is that the person does not appreciate himself, and is full of self-doubt and uncertainty. This can of course be a spur to achievement. Such a person can go for self-employment, that is freelance in some chosen field. There are many opportunities, only limited by the individual's choice. Salespeople and people who are working freelance maybe do not have the long Jupiter finger, but they do have one which juts out a bit, indicating that amount of aggression and push which are necessary to succeed in these fields.

Where a person is shy and not fond of the 'rat race' then a quiet but skilled job where the competitive aspect is non-existent would be most suitable. This is indicated in the hand by the first finger which does not lean or jut outwards.

Poor self-image, which causes more problems in people's lives than practically any other psychological thought pattern, is mostly formed in childhood by either real or fancied lack of parental love or approval. It may, of course, arise because of a physical defect which the person feels cuts him off from other people of his age. Again the obsession with some facial flaw may be a serious matter when it continues. Probably a philosophical approach is best; realize we are not the finished article, we are not perfect. If we were, we would not be here, we would be up with the angels or down with the devils according to some traditional religious teaching. We are none of us all-wise, all-knowing, all-beautiful; we all have our negative sides. Most of us try and work on these to improve ourselves and our relationships with others, plus of course our environment. In fact, in the end it comes down to a matter of our acceptance of ourselves, 'warts and all'. Cover-ups are not then so necessary and we have more energy for our work and play.

Are You Good With Your Hands? The Skilled Manual Worker

The person who possesses practical skills has the key to success — he is the saviour of today's society. This was probably always so, but the skilled worker was not valued as he should have been. People preferred the man who worked with his head rather than his hands, forgetting that the man who worked with his head actually had to have the skills of the manual worker in order to be able to run his own life successfully. Today, there are a multiplicity of machines which contribute to our efficiency, but also provide a rich field for those who are trained to look after them. We have washing-machines, dish-washers, hoovers and many other domestic machines. In the office, we have computers, typewriters, photocopiers and of course fax machines. Machines all need repairs and minders. The person who is good with his hands is in the happy position of knowing he will always be needed and so all his needs will be met financially.

As there are many and varied opportunities in this field, except where very specialist knowledge is required, many types of hand will involve themselves in gaining and using manual skills. Most people, though, will have arched fingerprints. These people really like to see what is wrong with a thing and get it back together again. Where the work is creative and so appeals to the person with creative ability you will often find the whorled fingerprint pattern.

Apart from machines there are of course lots of basic, necessary and very established fields into which those who like to work with their hands and can develop the necessary skills will flourish. These are in the areas of plumbing, carpentry, bricklaying, and dealing with electrics and gas. All these require engineering skills in the appropriate direction.

One thing which is easy to remember is that people with large hands are the ones found in fine, detailed work such as dentistry, jewellery-making and dispensing, while those with small hands are interested in large projects and engage in many different occupations.

Are You an Entertainer? Would You Like to Perform in Public?

The sign of the person who will be in some way in the public eye is shown by the hand with the fate line rising from Luna. This line does not confer talent, but I think it does show charm and charisma, the ability to get along with people and kindness. Perhaps the latter is the reason why they get along so well with others.

Apart from actually being an entertainer on the stage, there are other careers which come under the entertainment bracket. First and foremost of these is teaching and lecturing. This certainly brings the person before an audience. Politicians also have to get up before the public and, in Britain at least, put over their point of view to Parliament, and now cope with television as well, getting sort of double exposure.

It is of course necessary to communicate well to gravitate to this field and make a success of it. There is plenty of opportunity for communication in this day and age with the radio, television and the press.

We mentioned earlier that the air hand is the hand of the communicator, so it follows that the person with air type hands and with the fate line rising from Luna is a natural for this field.

We know that the third finger, the finger of Apollo or the Sun, is the finger of artistry. The sign of the artist, not necessarily purely in drawing or painting, is the long third finger with a whorl on its tip. I have found many talented cooks with whorls on the third finger. Their creation can be enjoyed and eaten. Their talent is stimulated by cooking materials rather than pen, paper and paints.

Musical talent is often shown by the development of the angles at the side of the thumb. I think it was Miss Hutchinson who mentioned the 'angle of perfect pitch'. The mount of Venus at the base of the thumb is not rounded, but angular, where this talent exists.

Pianists and organists usually have square tips to their fingers.

You will look to many different indications to build up the picture of an artist. You will look for the sensitive, more feminine type of hand with a soft skin, no knots on the joints and a particular linear pattern. Usually the Sun line will be evident, and head line will be sloping or long. The fingertips may well have the little droplets under them, which indicate a love of beauty. Taken together you have your picture of the artist.

Since the basic thing which an actor sets out to do is to communicate with his audience then it stands to reason the actor or actress will have an air hand with communicative skills well marked by long Apollo and Mercury fingers.

Writers are artists too, like the actor they deal with words. Their particular mark is the air hand with a head line which has a so-called 'writer's fork' on it.

Others who deal with the public are various consultants: lawyers, astrologers, palmists and magicians. All these people have to have an understanding of human nature, either through being born with it or acquiring it through the study of psychology, or again through the daily experience of dealing with many people. You will usually find the ring of Solomon on these hands, for it indicates the gift of understanding other people. Lawyers may also have the writer's fork mentioned above as it enables them to see both sides of the question. It used to be said that lawyers generally had a composite pattern on their Jupiter or first finger as this again enabled them to see both sides of a problem.

The Teacher

The teacher's hand is marked by the 'teacher's square' on the Jupiter mount. If the person is going to teach children, there should not be a wide gap between the head and life lines as this makes for impatience and would not therefore make for a successful teacher, lecturer or instructor.

The Worker in the Medical Field

The medical stigmata is the symbol of the person who wishes to help others and so will be drawn to a 'caring' profession, whether this is directly medical or social work.

Doctors have well-set-up hands, fairly large with long little fingers and long head lines. If the medical stigmata is missing on a doctor's hand you can be sure his choice of vocation was motivated more by money than by a desire to be of help to others.

Since the doctor needs to keep his cool his nervous system must be good, so his hands are short on lines.

Social workers usually also sport a medical stigmata, but the hands are more lined, less capable-looking.

Jobs Not Requiring a Specific Talent

There are many of these, including the clerical, secretarial and retailing industries and those in the field of production. Mr or Miss Average can fill one of these jobs without having to have a specific skill which would be marked on the hands. Unless there is some physical or psychological reason for not being able to work or hold down a job once it has been taken on, there is a whole range of work open to most people. The Civil Service, for instance, will suit many people as everything is set out and the future offered is secure.

If you are an employer, be wary of employing people

with widely-spaced fingers. They are independent and individualistic. They will fit nicely into your company if you require someone who thinks for themselves and you want them to think up bright ideas for you. Great, with a good incentive the person will suit you. However, if you want someone to toe the line and behave in a conventionally correct manner, pick someone whose fingers lie close together.

If you want your work or office well organized, do not pick someone with a short middle joint to their little finger, nor someone who has four joints to their little finger. These will produce muddle and mess for you as they are incapable of proper organization.

Also avoid people with very flexible thumbs. They are charming and great fun to be with, but businesslike they are not. Be a bit wary of the person with the clubbed thumb, for while this person will be quite normal and pleasant most of the time, there can be times when he or she will lose control and exhibit fits of anger which can lead to violence.

Think twice about employing someone with a simian line — this is where the two lines of heart and head are fused into one. The owner of the simian line is really very much a loner and often socially a misfit. If you want peace in your workforce, avoid employing the simian owner.

Where a person has many fine lines covering the palm of the hand, this person is an inveterate worrier with a sensitive nervous system and should never take on or be taken on in a job where there is a great deal of stress, or where the environment is stressful. These people find every little thing that goes wrong something to worry about and so are always in a state of tension bordering on distress.

Where the fate line is missing do not expect to keep these people. They are social misfits and also they have difficulty in sticking to a job as they have no real ambition or motivation, but live from day to day or week to week often simply to supply their drink, drug or tobacco habit.

You will see then that palmistry, while not a magic method of finding a suitable slot for everyone who consults for career advice, can nevertheless prove a most useful tool in helping to find the right career for the enquirer. Also in the analysis of the hand many things are sure to come to light which will illuminate different aspects of the character and so enable a person to know himself better. This understanding must be a help to a more fulfilling lifestyle.

Palmistry offers so much to the earnest student and enquirer, but it does demand quite a bit of concentrated study and effort in return. It opens a new window on life to those who are willing to persevere.

CHAPTER ELEVEN

HOW TO TAKE HAND OUTLINES AND PRINTS

Some of you may like to try your hand at taking either outlines of the hand or actual hand prints. The latter of course give more information than the former, but as the hand shape is the basic guide to character, the outlines will also be informative.

So for those of you who would like to try your hand at taking outlines, perhaps feeling that hand printing could be too difficult and messy, here's how.

Hand Outlines

First of all you need a table, a chair and a friend willing to be your 'victim'. On the table have a little pile of magazines to make a nice, soft, flexible, firm base for your paper, which should be of good quality A4. You also need a felt-tipped pen, black for preference. Ask your cooperative friend to shake one hand, making sure he is sitting comfortably and evenly on the chair. The hand which is going to be placed on the paper (which you will remember must be placed on the little pile of magazines), must be shaken from the wrist until it is absolutely relaxed. Now tell your friend to put his hand palm downwards on the paper and press it down adequately. Do *not* say *how* it should be put down, for the subject must choose how this should be done himself. Ask your friend to keep the hand very still once the position has been taken up, so that even when you come round with your pen to mark out the outlines of hand and fingers he should not try to accommodate you by shifting his fingers or thumb when he feels you marking out his hand outline. The difference between success and failure can be measured by the absolute stillness of the hands when you are doing this operation.

Remember to keep your felt-tipped pen upright as you outline the hand; keep as close to the hand as you can without squashing it. Mark some of the wrist, say half an inch, then, holding the paper, ask your subject to lift his hand off carefully as if he were peeling it off. If at first you don't succeed, try, try, try again, and you will.

At the top of your paper write in the person's name, date of birth and the date when you took the outline. If you want other details, such as colour or shape of nails, hands, texture of skin and size of the mounts, or fingerprint patterns, these should be noted at the head of the paper, as it adds to the information you can gain from the interpretation of the basic hand shape.

It is often easier in terms of time, mess and expertise to gain a few hand out lines as you start to study hands than it is to go in for full hand prints which are a bit more complex, and if you wanted to do them in style you would need to chase around for your equipment and spend a bit of money to finance your hobby.

How to Take a Print

You will need the same basics as you needed for taking the hand outlines — your willing friend and victim, your table, chair and A4 paper — and also some water-based lino printing ink. Black is the best colour as it makes the hands and the lines stand out well, but ink is often difficult to get in black, for some reason best known to the trade. The lino printing ink can be obtained at any art shop, where you can also get a 4-inch roller — if not you'll be able to pick up one in any photographic shop.

You will also need a square of non-porous material such as glass or perspex on which to put your blob of ink in order to be able to roll your ink onto your roller and so onto the palm of your hand.

Now, besides using the water-based lino printing ink, you can if you like use fingerprinting ink instead, but I don't advise it, as it is extremely messy and hard to get off; its shadow may well remain with your poor victim for quite a few days after the operation.

Many amateurs use lipstick, which is also messy and hard to get off and does not print well, for after all you are not going to use your best, most expensive lipstick to take prints.

Prior to starting your printing operation you will need to see that you have on your table a small pile of magazines, a few sheets of good quality A4 paper, a pen with which to outline your prints and to mark them, a 12-inch square of glass, formica or perspex, your tube of ink and your 4-inch roller.

Again you need to ask your friend to shake his hand, the one he is going to lay down on the paper when you have coated it evenly with the ink. In order to perform this operation you need to squeeze a small amount of ink, enough to cover a one-pence piece, on your square of glass (perspex, formica); you then roll your roller over this until the roller is evenly covered. Then coat your friend's hand evenly and ask him to place it on the A4 sheet. You now take your felt pen and, holding it upright, draw around the whole hand. Remember the subject must remain absolutely still throughout this operation.

Now we come to the crucial bit; when you have done this, tell your friend to raise his hand slightly without pulling it off the paper. You then put your right hand over the outside of your friend's hand and with your left hand push up gently but firmly against your own hand so that the 'well' which is so often missing in amateur prints comes out.

You then peel off the paper and repeat with the other hand. Take one or two prints as you may be very dissatisfied with the early efforts. There are many possibilities which may lead to disappointment, for instance, if the subject moves a hair's breadth while you are outlining the print, or if the subject has high mounts, then unless you do the maneouvre I just suggested, you will have a nasty white void in the centre of the print, instead of the lovely lines you had hoped to see.

Do make sure you have the ink well and evenly spread on the roller, for if you have a blot on one side and nothing on the other this is going to do very little for your imprint. Make sure your subject has relaxed his hand and has put it down on the paper according to his fancy. (This is an important point in interpretation.) Do not forget to outline the hand before you ask him to lift it up, without the paper falling away from his hand.

Another little point which will be helpful to you in interpretation is that after you have either taken the outline or the print, it does not matter which, you should really take a print or outline of the thumb. This is such an important pointer to the subject's character, intelligence, will power and health that you really need a separate picture of it.

To this end, if you are taking an outline, move the paper with the magazines underneath it to the edge of the table, then ask your subject to place his thumb along the edge of the table with the thumb pointed inward. Now outline the thumb.

If you are taking a print, again move the paper to the edge of the table, then ask your subject to hold up his thumb for you to cover it lightly with a little more water-based lino ink, then ask him to place the thumb at the edge of the table with the thumb pointing inwards. Again, outline the thumb.

You need to press down the thumb, as of course you also need to press down the hand lightly (although some people like to do their own pressing), but as the object of the exercise is to get good readable prints it is wise to see that all the instructions are followed as closely as possible.

Later, you can point your friends to the bathroom and say with pride that it will all come off easily with a little soap and water. Meanwhile you need to mark up your print as advised for the outlines and to take your equipment, wash it well and put it away in a little box or bag against the time when you will need to use it all again. Do see that the tube of ink is shut well or the ink will dry up and become difficult to use.

Even if you do not go on to take hand prints I hope that you will find interest and information in your reading of this book and any other books on hand reading which you study.

INDEX